BUSINESS
WITHOUT THE
BULLSH*T

ALSO BY GEOFFREY JAMES

How to Say It: Business to Business Selling
Scientific Selling (coauthor)
Success Secrets from Silicon Valley
Business Wisdom of the Electronic Elite
The Tao of Programming
The Zen of Programming
Computer Parables
Document Databases

BUSINESS WITHOUT THE BULLSH*T

49 SECRETS AND SHORTCUTS YOU NEED TO KNOW

Geoffrey James

BUSINESS PLUS

NEW YORK   BOSTON

Business Plus
Hachette Book Group
237 Park Avenue
New York, NY 10017

HachetteBookGroup.com

Printed in the United States of America

RRD-C

First Edition: May 2014
10 9 8 7 6 5 4 3 2

Business Plus is an imprint of Grand Central Publishing.
The Business Plus name and logo are trademarks of Hachette Book Group, Inc.

The publisher is not responsible for websites (or their content) that are not owned by the publisher.

Library of Congress Cataloging-in-Publication Data
James, Geoffrey.
   Business without the bullsh*t : 49 secrets and shortcuts you need to know / Geoffrey James. — First edition.
       pages cm
     ISBN 978-1-4555-7458-2 (hardback) — ISBN 978-1-4555-7457-5 (ebook) — ISBN 978-1-4789-5355-5 (audio download)   1. Career development.
2. Management.   3. Corporate culture.   4. Psychology, Industrial.
5. Success in business.   I. Title.
   HF5381.J44 2014
   650.1—dc23
                                                                    2013038653

For Cordelia and Alexander

Contents

CONTENTS

Introduction

For the past thirty years, I've been on a quest to discover tactics and techniques that cut through the business world's bullsh*t and help you get things done more quickly and easily than you ever thought possible.

As a journalist I've interviewed hundreds of executives, ranging from living legends to unknown entrepreneurs struggling with their initial start-ups, as well as dozens of sales and marketing gurus. As an engineer and marketer I've participated in the growth of a wildly productive organization and observed—firsthand and up close—as two huge companies disintegrated under the weight of their own collective stupidity.

For the past seven years I've had daily conversations about surviving and thriving in the corporate world with the millions of readers of my blog, which has appeared on BNET and the CBS News website, and is currently on Inc.com.

*Business Without the Bullsh*t* is the result of that quest.

This is not a book of theory. It's a collection of practical approaches to the real-life situations that take place every day inside just about every company.

There is, however, an underlying philosophy about business and bullsh*t that underpins this entire book. You can use this book without knowing that philosophy, but for readers who appreciate context, here goes:

EVERYONE IS A FREELANCER

In the past, most businesspeople worked for a specific company and often expected to work for that company for decades. Some firms even touted a policy of "lifetime" employment.

In those days there was an implicit contract between employer and employee. The employer offered job security and in return the employee was loyal. Employers looked askance at a prospective employee who hopped from job to job.

At the very bottom of the corporate totem pole were freelancers and consultants, the losers who couldn't land a real job and were thus reduced to constantly selling and reselling their services.

That world is gone forever. Rather than offering job security, companies now move jobs wherever they can be done more cheaply. Similarly, those who stick with one employer for too long now seem out of touch or lacking in initiative.

Today everyone is a freelancer. Even if you've got a salaried position with benefits, perks, paid vacations, and a fancy title, you're still a freelancer. If you aren't constantly selling and reselling your services, you'll be unemployed faster than you can say *pink slip*.

This means that, above all else, you must not just keep your options open but actively and constantly develop new job opportunities. As a freelancer, your goal must always be to land your next job, hopefully one that's more fun and pays better than the one you've already got.

YOU ARE YOUR BOSS

Inherent in the obsolete notion of job security is a management hierarchy: you work for a boss, who works for a bigger boss, who works for the CEO, who works for the board of directors, which works for the investors.

While that structure still exists in the corporate world, when you're a freelancer, it no longer makes sense to think of yourself as "being managed" by somebody else. A boss is more like a client or customer, which means you must manage the relationship.

Similarly, the old concepts of what it means to be the boss are increasingly meaningless. Your employees—the ones who are smart and therefore "get" that they're freelancers—aren't going to fall in line just because you've got a job title.

That's just the start. As a freelancer you must be capable of managing not just upward and downward, but sideways as well. You must influence and convince your coworkers to help you achieve your goals, usually by helping them achieve theirs.

Finally, and most important, you must learn to manage inwardly, controlling your thoughts, habits, and actions so they serve your greater purpose.

YOU MUST SELL YOURSELF

Because you're now a freelancer and your own boss, you're also a salesperson, whether you want to be one or not.

If you can't (or won't) sell yourself, your services, and your ideas, you might as well give up now. If you're not unemployed already, you will be soon. And you'll probably stay that way.

Despite this, a surprising number of people are reluctant to learn how to sell, probably because popular culture views the process of selling with a combination of disdain, distrust, and disgust.

In nearly every movie, play, and television show in which they appear as characters, salespeople are depicted as slick-talking con men or pitiful sad sacks. This prejudice against selling extends into academia, where only a handful of colleges teach Sales in their business schools.

The truth is that selling is, and always has been, the soul of business. Companies that can't sell their products go bankrupt. Even nonprofits and government agencies depend entirely on *somebody's* ability to sell the usefulness of whatever service those organizations provide.

If you want true career security, learn to sell.

CLARITY CREATES POWER

Since you're going to be managing other people (upward, downward, and sideways) and selling your value to them daily, your most important management and selling skill is the ability to make yourself understood.

In the past, being obtuse carried some business value. While engineers and scientists were expected to communicate with precision, businesspeople often found it useful to blur issues. "You can't pin Jell-O to the wall," as the saying went.

Today, however, we live and work in a world of massive information overload. According to McKinsey, the average corporate worker sends and receives over a hundred e-mails daily, an activity that consumes nearly a third of every workday.

To make matters worse, the inexorable juggernauts of globalization and computerization have made the business of business more complex. As a result, whatever value once resided in bureaucratic double-talk has long departed.

In an information-rich world, the real challenge is to simplify what's complex, without being simplistic. Whoever does this well commands vast power over those who otherwise would be drowning in the endless sea of information.

PEOPLE TRUMP TECHNOLOGY

For decades high-tech firms have touted the absurd notion that technology, by itself, solves problems. Technology only increases the speed with which humans perform selected activities, an increase that may either solve problems or create new ones.

For example, when first introduced into corporations, e-mail was supposed to improve productivity. Where it had once taken an hour to type and distribute a memo, one could now, with e-mail, do the same task in mere minutes.

Unfortunately, while some people used the convenience of e-mail to reduce the time spent writing memos, others used the same convenience to increase the number of memos they send, contributing to information overload.

While we may be technologically more sophisticated, the human behaviors in the modern corporation—building alliances, recruiting mentors, selling ideas, and so forth—are identical to those found in every period of history.

Thus, while it's valuable to understand how to use today's technology, an ability to create value emerges from understanding other people, discovering what motivates them, and learning how to satisfy their individual needs.

Because of this, my book focuses on human beings and human behaviors rather than on technology. While I discuss techniques for social media and e-mail, for instance, the emphasis is on using such technologies to influence other people.

COURAGE IS CRUCIAL

As you read this book, you may sometimes find it difficult to imagine yourself following some of the advice or attempting to replicate the sample conversations. Such feelings are a signal that you *must* follow the advice.

For example, suppose you're frightened by the idea of interrupting a yelling boss, insisting that he treat you professionally, and then walking out if he refuses to comply. Your fear shows a predisposition to be a victim.

Since that's true, the only way you can prevent yourself from actually becoming a victim is to take actions that make you uncomfortable even when you are simply reading about them. And that takes courage.

Courage is not the same as being fearless. Only fools are fearless. Courage means taking risks to get what you want. Courage means facing the reality that if you stand up for yourself, you might lose your job.

In this book I explain how to lay the groundwork to ensure that you not only don't lose your job but are constantly positioned for a better one. But all the advice in the world is useless unless you can summon the courage to follow it.

BELIEFS DRIVE RESULTS

In the previous paragraphs I attempt to redefine, or at least ask you to question, common beliefs about the workplace, your role in it, and the nature of your work relationships.

I'm doing this because beliefs determine whether or not you'll be, or can be, successful in business. To be successful you must differentiate between facts, which are pieces of reality, and beliefs, which are only your interpretation of what that reality *means*.

Your beliefs, not the facts, determine how well (or badly) you'll perform in any given situation. To illustrate this point, suppose the economy is growing very slowly. The economy is a fact. Your beliefs come into play when you decide what that fact means to you.

For example, one person might interpret a slow economy as meaning that "it will be nearly impossible for me to find a job." That's a belief. Another person might interpret a slow economy as meaning that "companies need my help more than ever." That's also a belief.

The same exact fact can thus generate two opposing beliefs. Which is "true"? It doesn't matter. What does matter is that the person who's convinced finding a job will be nearly impossible is far less likely to find one, or interview well for it, than the person who's convinced she's needed now more than ever.

The business world is full of challenges. Sometimes the game is rigged. Sometimes people do weird things. Sometimes deals go sour. Sometimes your plans don't pan out.

So what? Stuff happens. However, you're far more likely to pick yourself up, try again, and ultimately succeed if you adopt beliefs that help you remain optimistic, enthusiastic, and positive.

This does not mean being blind to reality or looking at the world through Pollyanna glasses. It simply means choosing beliefs that let you interpret reality in a way that helps you achieve the results you want.

BUSINESS IS SIMPLE

Conventional wisdom is that business is complicated and its principles difficult to master. However, while every industry and every profession requires specific expertise, the business of business tends to be rather simple.

Unfortunately, the livelihood of hundreds of thousands of management consultants, industry analysts, and corporate trainers depends on keeping things complex—because, after all, once you realize that business is simple, why would you hire them?

Beyond your own area of expertise, all you need to be truly successful in the business world is a handful of secrets and shortcuts. There's no mystery to being successful. It is truly within your grasp.

And that's what this book is all about. I've gathered together the most effective techniques and tactics that I've discovered in my lifelong quest. And I've made them as simple and easy to understand as I possibly could.

HOW TO READ THIS BOOK

Business Without the Bullsh*t isn't intended to be read from cover to cover, as you might read a novel or a traditional business book. Instead, it contains lists of advice and step-by-step plans to handle specific situations.

You can therefore turn to any chapter (or secret, as I call them) and immediately apply the techniques. Each chapter also includes a "shortcut"—a quick reminder that encapsulates the secret at a glance.

While each secret can be learned and applied separately, I've grouped them so related secrets are presented together. For example, "How to Land a Job Interview" is followed immediately by "How to Ace a Job Interview."

Overall, each group or part of the book covers a different facet of your business life, so you can read and use that part when it's most useful to the current stage of your career.

I start by explaining how to manage your boss because, based on the comments I receive from my blog readers, that's the most pressing need. I then expand outward to managing coworkers and employees, and then inward to managing yourself and your own career.

The first four parts thus provide what you need to know to get the most out of everyone you work with, including yourself.

The fifth part presents tools you'll need to achieve clarity and sell your ideas and the value of your services. The sixth and seventh parts handle special situations that might otherwise throw you off track.

One final thing. Much of the wisdom in this book emerged from comments and e-mails sent to me by the readers of my blog. I'd therefore be remiss if I didn't offer to give back. If you e-mail me with a question or a comment (gj@geoffreyjames.com), I'll absolutely answer as best I can.

This book is for you.

PART I

How to Manage Your Boss

It would be nice to imagine that the success of your career rests upon your competence at doing your job, but that's less than half the picture. Raises, promotions, and other perks depend directly on how well you can manage your boss.

If he or she doesn't warm to you—or worse, doesn't remember that you exist—you'll never land the plum assignments you need to get ahead. And if your boss dislikes you, you're in for a difficult time until you find another position or get another boss.

The key to managing a boss is not to envision that boss as an overseer or as a commanding officer. That's not appropriate because the relationship between boss and employee is symbiotic: to be successful, each of you needs the other.

Think of your boss as providing a service that helps you get your job done. Your boss secures the resources you need, makes decisions when there's disagreement, works interdepartmental issues, and secures money to get you a raise.

This part of the book provides you with everything you really need to know about managing upward:

■ "The Twelve Types of Bosses" describes the generic varieties of boss, their typical management styles, and a general idea of how to manage them so they do what you'd prefer.

■ "How to Keep Any Boss Happy" explains what bosses—regardless of type—expect from you as an individual. There are eight rules here, but the eighth is by far the most important.

■ "How to Get the Best from Your Boss" contains a step-by-step plan to make certain the boss knows all the things you're doing right, while you also build personal rapport so the boss keeps your best interests in mind.

■ "How to Use Your Performance Review" shows the best way to turn your regular performance review into an opportunity to create career momentum and lay the groundwork for a future raise or promotion.

■ "How to Ask for a Raise" builds on the concepts in the previous secret so you can approach the challenge of asking for money in such a way that it feels both natural and inevitable to the boss that you should be paid more than you're currently being paid.

■ "How to Handle Unreasonable Requests" helps you negotiate those uncomfortable situations that arise when your boss demands more of you than you can possibly deliver, or asks you to do something that would damage your career.

■ "How to Cope with a Bully" provides a step-by-step approach for defusing bosses who act inappropriately and unprofessionally. Hopefully this won't happen to you often, but knowing what to do is a good skill to have.

The Twelve Types of Bosses

During your career you'll need to work with and for a variety of different bosses. To do this effectively, you need to know approximately where each boss is "coming from" in terms of management style.

Over the years I've gotten to know and work with dozens of bosses (and heard complaints about thousands more), and it's become clear to me that there are twelve types, each of which must be handled in a slightly different way.

This secret serves as a field guide to understanding the types of bosses that you'll encounter and the overall strategy you'll need to manage each one. Later in this section, I'll provide you more detailed tactics to work within those strategies.

1. THE VISIONARY

Visionaries are more concerned with the future than with what's going on here and now. They manage by creating (or trying to create) a reality-distortion field that makes people believe the visionary and his team can accomplish the impossible.

Many visionary bosses view the late Steve Jobs as a role model, and that's the problem. Like Jobs, visionary bosses can be intolerant, overly critical, and unfair, and sometimes throw tantrums when they don't get their way.

Not surprisingly, visionaries are most commonly found inside high-tech and biotech firms. When they migrate into traditional industries, they usually end up returning to their original spawning ground.

If you're working for a visionary, be willing to drink the Kool-Aid, work ridiculously long hours, and listen to endless variations of "this product is going to *change the WORLD*." If that's your cup of tea, this type of boss can be a lot of fun, tantrums and all.

2. THE CLIMBER

Climbers are all about getting themselves promoted. As a general rule they're interested in you as an employee only insofar as you can help or hinder their ascent to the corner office.

Climbers are master politicians. They never have colleagues; only competitors. They spend endless time and effort figuring out how to win status, claim credit, and build alliances.

With climbers you must be clear in your own mind that loyalty is simply not part of the relationship, and that you'll be discarded faster than a month-old mackerel the second you make the climber look bad.

With that proviso, if you're working for a climber, do what you can to make him look good and (most important) be the person who has his back when his fellow climbers try to stab it.

3. THE BUREAUCRAT

Bureaucrats believe that their position and importance lies in an ability to make everything run by the book. They are resistant to change because they see the current situation (which is the one that put them in power) as the best of all possible worlds.

In the olden days, bureaucrats used to love endless pages of paperwork. Today they love endless screens of online forms. They also love meetings, especially those that review and discuss the activities of others.

Bureaucrats thrive inside what they like to call "large enterprises." They falter in small firms because the lack of a crowd makes it too obvious that they aren't really doing very much.

Bureaucrats are predictable and easy to please. Document everything in detail and limit all your activities to what's been done in the past, even if it no longer works. Warning: a bureaucrat boss can grind your creativity into dust.

4. THE PROPELLERHEAD

When engineers get into the management chain, they bring a technology-oriented worldview with them. This is not necessarily a bad thing, but it does mean you'll be judged almost entirely on your technical competence.

The propellerhead boss prefers employees who are experts in some technical field—the more obscure the better. They consider all nontechnical types (like MBA holders) equally stupid and useless.

Don't take offense if a propellerhead boss communicates with you primarily through e-mail, even if that boss has an office two cubicles away. Propellerheads tend to avoid people issues.

The easiest way to get on the good side of a propellerhead is to become fluent in nerdy pop culture references. If possible, illustrate your business point by quoting lines from *Star Trek* or *Star Wars*.

5. THE FOGEY

These bosses have been around since the days when "secretaries" (whoever they were) used "typewriters" (whatever they were). Fogeys are simultaneously wise in the ways of the world and clueless about what's actually going on.

Fogeys who are close to retirement are often quite jovial and easy-going; those who must continue to work because they can't afford to retire can be meaner than dyspeptic weasels.

Working for a fogey requires the patience to listen to the same "war stories" multiple times. Don't assume the duffer is a doofus, though. Fogeys can be surprisingly shrewd, especially when it comes to political infighting.

Fogeys are mostly looking for two things: respect from the young'uns, and reassurance that they're still relevant. They make great mentors, because they tend to be generous with their advice and time.

6. THE WHIPPERSNAPPER

The flip side of the fogey is the barely-out-of-college go-getter who's assigned to manage a group of seasoned employees. Whippersnappers are energetic, enthusiastic, and secretly afraid that nobody is taking them seriously.

Because that insecurity is so huge, follow two essential rules when working for whippersnappers: (1) respond positively to the energy they bring to their job; and (2) never, ever remind them of their relative inexperience.

Needless to say, you may end up wasting time repairing problems generated by the whippersnapper's inexperience. That's fine, but remember to be *enthusiastic* about it! However, depending on your level of tolerance for the whippersnapper's learning curve, you may want to consider finding work elsewhere.

7. THE SOCIAL DIRECTOR

Social directors see management as a community-building process. They consider the personal interactions that happen in the work-place as important as (and sometimes more important than) the actual work itself.

Social directors always try to manage by consensus. They call a LOT of meetings and spend a LOT of time letting people air their opinions and ideas. They shy away from making decisions that might leave a team member "disappointed."

Working for a social director requires you to constantly build alliances and garner supporters. If you want a decision to be made, you'll need to get everybody on the team to back it publicly.

A word of warning: when it comes to handling their own emotions, social directors can be pressure cookers. They either let off steam through a series of hissy fits, or they suddenly explode. If it's the latter, try to be elsewhere when it happens.

8. THE DICTATOR

This is the classic "It's my way or the highway" boss. While most people find this management style grating, working for a dictator has some advantages. They make decisions quickly and efficiently, without over-analyzing everything.

Another advantage of working for a dictator is knowing exactly where you stand. Why should your boss bother to stab you in the back when it's more convenient to stab you in the front?

Unfortunately, dictators tend to be impervious to outside opinion and brittle when it comes to change. When they fail (and they always fail eventually), it's on a truly epic scale.

The tricks to working for a dictator are (1) follow orders, (2) follow orders, and (3) be ready to jump to another job when you see the dictator driving your company (or your division) over the cliff.

9. THE SALES STAR

Selling is part of every job, and every boss should be able to sell his or her ideas up and down the management chain. The problem with this type of boss is that selling is the only thing he or she does well.

These bosses are usually created when top sales professionals are promoted into management. This happens with fair frequency, despite the fact that managing people requires a different skill set than selling to customers.

Sales star bosses tend to be self-motivated, aggressive, and good at building relationships, understanding needs, and generating workable solutions. That's because they're salespeople.

Therefore, the way to deal with sales stars is to encourage them to sell! Bring them into situations where a deal must be closed, or terms negotiated. They'd really rather be getting their hands dirty (as it were) than managing people anyway.

10. THE HATCHET MAN

Hatchet men (or women) are brought into an organization to fire people as quickly as possible, usually to make the company more attractive to investors or position it for an acquisition.

By the very nature of the job, such bosses aren't likely to be filled with the proverbial milk of human kindness. Still, being human, they can't resist euphemisms that cast their actions in a positive light (e.g., *corporate triage* and *ventilating the firm*).

There are only two roles available for people who work for a hatchet man: henchman and victim. Ultimately the favored role, that of henchman, is temporary: they often get canned too.

The best way to deal with a hatchet man is to be long gone by the time he arrives. This requires attention to the writing on the wall. For example, the moment you see the words *private equity investment* on an internal memo, your new job is finding a new job. (See "Secret 39. What to Do If There's a Layoff.")

11. THE LOST LAMB

Sometimes people who have no management talent end up in a position of authority. This generally happens when a manager leaves suddenly and top management needs somebody to hold the fort while it finds a replacement.

Lost lambs have no idea what to do other than continue whatever policies and strategies were previously in place. They know they're placeholders and dread doing anything that will be held against them once they're pushed back into the ranks.

What these bosses want is for you to move your projects forward without bringing ANY difficult decisions to them. They are, however, easily convinced to make minor decisions in your favor simply to keep you happy.

The biggest danger with a lost lamb is that if you end up making the lamb too successful, top management may conclude that the temporary assignment should be permanent, and you'll be saddled with the dead weight of the lost lamb for the foreseeable future.

12. THE HERO

There are indeed men and women in this world whose personalities and characters make them well suited to manage other people. They're the fabled "natural leaders," and they're as rare as diamonds in dunghills.

Heroes prefer to coach others than to do things themselves. They have a knack for figuring out exactly what their employees need in order to do a superlative job and then how to get that for them.

Heroes always give their teams credit for the wins but take personal responsibility for the losses. They believe that "the buck stops here" not that "sh*t rolls downhill."

There are two problems with working for a hero. The first is that the hero will probably get promoted or be recruited to work elsewhere. The second is that once you've worked for a hero, it ruins your ability to work for a bozo.

THE TWELVE TYPES OF BOSSES

- **VISIONARIES** are inspiring assholes so drink the Kool-Aid.

- **CLIMBERS** want to get ahead so expect no loyalty.

- **BUREAUCRATS** hate change so document everything.

- **PROPELLERHEADS** love gadgets so become an expert.

- **FOGEYS** want respect so recruit them as mentors.

- **WHIPPERSNAPPERS** are insecure so be enthusiastic!

- **SOCIAL DIRECTORS** love consensus but may explode.

- **DICTATORS** make fast decisions but cause disasters.

- **SALES STARS** would rather be selling so let them sell.

- **HATCHET MEN** execute layoffs so leave now.

- **LOST LAMBS** need your help but may get dependent.

- **HEROES** are rare so enjoy them while it lasts.

How to Keep Any Boss Happy

Regardless of the type of boss you're working with, they all want and need the same things. Unfortunately, bosses are not always all that good at articulating these needs, which is why I list them here—so you know what's expected.

1. KEEP YOUR PROMISES.

Your boss wants to trust you. Really. Your boss wants to trust you to get your job done, so everyone else (including the boss) doesn't get left in the lurch. That trust, however, is possible only if you keep your promises.

Therefore, whenever you accept an assignment, follow through religiously, even fanatically. Do what you say you're going to do. Never over-commit, and avoid hedging your bets with vague statements like "I'll try" and "Maybe."

More than anything else, you want your boss to see you as reliable. When you make your word carry real weight, you lighten the load of worry upon your boss's shoulders, making his or her job much easier.

2. NO SURPRISES, EVER.

What keeps every boss awake at night is the secret fear that employees are screwing up but aren't saying anything about it, hoping that the disaster will go away before it becomes a train wreck.

Even if you're afraid some bad news might upset your boss, don't wait until the last minute to deliver it. (Note, though, as explained below, your report of a problem should always include your best attempt at a solution.)

This rule is essential when you've got the kind of boss who consistently "shoots the messenger" when surprised with bad news. To avoid "being shot," give your boss constant updates on your projects before they metastasize into huge problems.

3. TAKE YOUR JOB SERIOUSLY.

Your boss doesn't expect you to be perfect, but bosses appreciate employees who truly care about what they do and are willing to take the time to do a job well and thoroughly.

Very few things irritate bosses more than employees who affect a flippant attitude toward work. Having a sense of humor about the problems you encounter is a good thing; making snarky remarks is not.

Bosses are particularly annoyed by employees who treat work as an extension of their personal lives. I recently heard a story about an intern who thought it was appropriate to bring her boyfriend into the office to sit and talk with her as she worked. Ouch!

4. ADVISE, THEN OBEY.

When your boss needs to make a decision, he or she depends on you to provide advice and perspective, especially in areas that are in your particular bailiwick. Indeed, providing such advice is the best way for you to ensure that the best decision is made.

When you see your boss about to make a foolish decision, it's also your responsibility to attempt to convince him or her to make a better one. Make your best case, and express yourself clearly.

However, once your boss has made a decision, stop second-guessing and do your best to implement it—regardless of whether you think that decision was the best one possible. After all, maybe your boss knows more than you do.

5. PROVIDE SOLUTIONS, NOT COMPLAINTS.

Nothing is more irritating (or more boring) to a boss than listening to somebody kvetch about things that either they're not willing to change or are outside the boss's ability to change.

As a general rule, never bring up a problem unless you have a solution to propose or are asking for the boss's advice. If the latter, take your boss's advice without adding a "Yeah, but..." argument.

If you're proposing a solution, your boss would far prefer that the solution be something *you* plan on doing, rather than something you'd like the boss to do for you. Bosses hate it when employees "upwardly delegate."

6. COMMUNICATE CLEARLY.

Bosses have neither the time nor the inclination to wade through piles of biz-blab, jargon, and weasel words. This is true even when bosses are themselves unable to communicate without using these verbal crutches.

When dealing with your boss, speak and write in short sentences, use the fewest words possible to make a point, and make that point easily understandable. (See "Secret 29. Five Rules for Business Communication.")

When you communicate clearly, you not only make your boss's job easier, you make it easier for your boss to communicate what you're doing (and why) to other powers that be, such as the CEO.

7. DO YOUR BEST WORK.

Bosses expect you to do your absolute best at whatever job you undertake. They expect you to overcome obstacles and difficulties that would prevent most people from succeeding at your job.

Fortunately, it's very much in your own interest to excel at your job, because scuttlebutt travels so quickly. In today's hyper-connected business world, everyone inside your company (and outside too) will eventually find out whether you do your job well.

In the same way that the quality of a product creates that product's brand image, the quality of your work creates your reputation. More important, that reputation—immortalized on the Web—now follows you around forever.

8. MAKE YOUR BOSS SUCCESSFUL.

Regardless of what it says on your job description, *your real job is to make your boss successful.* It doesn't matter what type of boss you're working for, rest assured that there are *no* exceptions to this rule.

SHORTCUT

MAKING YOUR BOSS HAPPY

- **DO** what you say you'll do.
- **KEEP** your boss in the loop.
- **CARE** about your quality of work.
- **ACCEPT** decisions when they're made.
- **SOLVE** problems without whining.
- **BE** concise and clear.
- **DO** the best work you can.
- **IMPORTANT:** Make your boss successful.

How to Get the Best from Your Boss

Now that you know what your boss expects of you, let's examine how to put your boss to work for you by moving your career forward and looking out for your interests. Here's how:

1. EXPLAIN HOW YOU PREFER TO BE MANAGED.

Sometime during your first conversations with your boss (and ideally before you agree to work for that boss), explain to that boss what kind of management style works best for you, personally.

Deciding what works for you requires some self-reflection. If you've been in the workplace for a while, you may have been exposed to different management styles. If so, recall what management behaviors got your best work from you.

If you're starting out in business, draw from your educational experience. Which of your teachers really inspired you and why? Which of them were difficult to learn from?

Another way to understand your preferences in this area is to ask yourself some questions:

- Do you like public praise or does it make you uncomfortable?

- Does criticism leave you with hurt feelings or do you generally shrug it off?
- Do you prefer being told what you're doing right rather than what you're doing wrong?

Your goal is to discover enough about yourself and what you need that you can articulate clearly how you can best be managed. If you don't, you'll inevitably receive whatever one-size-fits-all management style your boss finds most familiar.

The best time to communicate your preferences is during your first meeting with your boss. If you're already working for a boss, the best time is your next one-on-one meeting. Don't put it off! The clearer you communicate what you need, the better the relationship you'll have, to the ultimate benefit of both you and your boss.

2. OVER-PREPARE FOR EVERY MEETING.

Most bosses live in constant fear they'll be blindsided by incompetence. To reassure themselves, bosses often pick an aspect of an employee's job and begin randomly asking questions about the details.

If you think this means you're on trial when this happens to you, it's because you are. Answer these queries with grace and aplomb and your boss will assume you're competent. Hesitate or evade and your boss will assume all your work is slipshod.

Since you don't know in advance which questions your boss might ask, be prepared for every contingency. Plan on about an hour of prep for every hour with your direct boss, two hours for every hour with your boss's boss, and so forth up the management chain.

3. REMIND YOUR BOSS WHY YOU'RE VALUABLE.

Even the best bosses tend to forget things. They usually have plenty on their minds and may not even know what you're working on, much less what a fabulous job you're doing.

Worst case, this failure to communicate could result in you achieving goals and objectives that are no longer the boss's priorities. If that happens, all your hard work will likely be seen as wasted efforts rather than accomplishments.

To prevent this, create a "core message" that lets the boss know what you're doing, and work that message into every conversation, even if it's only a hallway chat.

Examples:

- "The recruiting program I set up is putting us in touch with some very qualified candidates."
- "We just ran my power-management module through an entire suite of accuracy and stress tests."
- "My negotiation with Acme Corp. is taking a while, but I think I'll be able to get the favorable terms we wanted."

4. CULTIVATE YOUR BOSS'S PEERS.

You may *think* you have a one-on-one relationship with your boss, but you're actually part of a crowd of people—from your peers to your customers to those who influence the boss's decision-making.

When it comes to evaluating your performance, your boss listens to the opinions of others in the company. Therefore, it's not enough to simply inform your boss what you're doing. If you want to advance your career and your personal agenda, you must ensure that the other people spread the word.

Create a list of people who influence your boss and compose a variation of your core message for each of them.

For example, suppose you're in a marketing group working on the development of sales channels (people who don't work for your company but who sell your product). Your messages might be:

- For your boss (VP of marketing): "I'm developing a channel sales program that will recruit new resellers." (This is your core message.)
- For the VP of engineering: "My channel sales program will get your products into the hands of new customers."
- For the VP of manufacturing: "With the channel sales program I'm developing, we'll be able to better predict how many products you'll need to build."
- For the VP of human resources: "The channel sales program I'm developing will let us increase revenue without hiring more people."
- For the CFO: "With the channel sales program I'm developing, we'll get a twenty percent higher gross margin than through direct sales."
- For the CEO: "My boss, [name], has me working on a channel sales program that could improve our overall profitability by several percent."

5. SHOW INTEREST IN YOUR BOSS'S CAREER.

Once you've convinced the boss that you're competent, it's time to make yourself invaluable. To do this you'll need to deliver what your boss wants—even before your boss knows he or she wants it.

Over time, of course, you can observe and learn, but it's smarter to get things moving more quickly by asking questions that will help you understand your boss's way of thinking. As a side benefit, your boss may be flattered that you're interested.

Use the Internet, the grapevine, and the boss's admin to learn about the boss's work history. When appropriate, find opportunities (such as during lunch or off-site meetings) to express a healthy curiosity about your boss's experience.

Apart from the fact that most people enjoy talking about themselves, bosses find this kind of inquiry valuable because it provides them with opportunities to explain the logic of their decision-making processes.

Examples:

- "I was on the Web learning more about our industry and I noticed that you presented at [name of event]. I'm curious: what response did you get?"
- "Your admin mentioned you used to work for [name of firm]. I'm curious: what's the most valuable thing you learned from that experience?"
- "I hear you used to work in the [name] industry. I'm curious: what are the main differences between the way that industry works and the way ours works?"

6. CULTIVATE COMPATIBLE PERSONAL INTERESTS.

The ideal situation is to have a boss who looks out for your interests even during difficult times. This protectiveness is nurtured when the boss thinks of you not just as competent but as a kindred spirit.

Therefore, if you want a better relationship with your boss, it never hurts to cultivate an interest in (and maybe some enthusiasm for) something that also interests your boss. Ideally this should be an interest or activity that segues nicely into the work experience.

For example, if your boss likes to talk business while playing golf, learn to play. If your boss loves science fiction, ask which books are his or her favorites and then read them. If you think about it, you do this kind of thing all the time in your other relationships. Why not for the boss?

Your goal is to get to know the boss without being creepy or smarmy. It helps if you remember that bosses are human and, as such, truly want you to understand what makes them tick.

SHORTCUT

GETTING YOUR BOSS WORKING FOR YOU

- **COMMUNICATE** what you need in order to do your best.

- **KEEP** your manager informed of your progress.

- **MAKE** a case that you're doing a useful job.

- **ENSURE** that everyone knows how you contribute.

- **UNDERSTAND** your boss's goals and desires.

- **FIND** and cultivate a common interest.

How to Use Your Performance Review

Most people treat performance reviews much as students treat report cards—as a way to find out how well they did when it's too late to do anything about it. That's naive, because your performance review is not a report card but a tool for you to get what you want.

If handled correctly (as shown below) the "review" part of this process will be either a formality or a victory lap. Then you use the meeting to set expectations for the future and extract promises that will advance your career.

1. ASK HOW YOU'LL BE MEASURED AND REWARDED.

Every time you get a new boss or after you read this, schedule a one-on-one meeting with him or her as soon as possible. Ask the following questions:

1. What are your expectations of me over the next year?
2. How will you measure whether I've fulfilled them?
3. If I exceed those metrics, what do I get?

Your goal is to get your boss to be as specific as possible on all three points. If you do not have this conversation, when your next performance review comes around, you will be blindsided, because you've only been guessing what's expected of you and assuming what reward you'll get.

Whenever your boss makes you a promise, listen carefully to how that promise is worded. It's one thing for a boss to say, "Do this and I'll promote you" (which seldom happens), and quite another for a boss to say, "Do this and you *might* get a promotion."

Whenever you hear vagueness in a promise, ask a question that, if answered truthfully, will remove that vagueness. Example:

- *Boss*: Complete project A by August and you'll be in line for a promotion.
- *You*: Assuming I do so, what's the likelihood of the promotion on a scale of one to ten, with ten being a sure thing?

If the boss can't or won't provide specifics, you can assume whatever promise is being made is meaningless. In business, a promise is only a commitment when it has measurable details connected to it.

Take detailed notes on the conversation. Afterward, send an e-mail to your boss thanking him or her for being so helpful, and also documenting the specific commitments made on both sides.

If you fail to document the conversation, there is a very good chance that, come performance review time, your boss will have changed how you're being measured and forgotten whatever promises were made.

2. PERIODICALLY COMPARE ACHIEVEMENTS TO METRICS.

Throughout the year, send update e-mails to your boss, based on your original "here's our agreement" e-mail, documenting both how you've been tracking against the boss's expectations and the metrics by which those expectations are being measured.

These updates are essential because they force you to pay constant attention to exceeding the agreed-upon metrics and keep you from being distracted by side issues. The updates also force your boss to explicitly state whether and how the metrics have changed in response to changes in business conditions.

If your boss changes the expectations or the metrics, set up another one-on-one—ostensibly to discuss the new expectations and metrics, but actually to make it clear that you still expect to be rewarded based on whatever work you've already accomplished.

This is important because bosses sometimes change employee metrics in order to avoid fulfilling commitments. For example, a sales manager might promise you a bonus if you beat your quota, and then raise your quota when you're about to beat it.

Example 1:

> *Boss:* You'll now be measured on the profitability of the company rather than the amount of usable computer code you produce.
>
> *You:* I understand the new metric. However, I've outperformed our agreed-upon metrics for nine months now, so I expect to get a raise, regardless of our company's financial performance.

Example 2:

> *Boss:* We're changing your sales quota so that it's fifty percent larger for the current year.
>
> *You:* I will try my best to beat that goal! However, I expect my bonus to be paid based on my outperforming of the current quota.

3. WRITE THE DRAFT OR PROVIDE "INPUTS."

Most bosses hate writing performance reviews. You've already made the job easier with your periodic reports, so it only makes sense for you to offer to take that burden off your boss's shoulders and onto your own.

Most bosses will be more than happy to let you write the draft. If your boss demurs, do it anyway, but send your draft as "inputs" to your performance review, which is much the same thing.

As you write the draft (or "inputs"), stick to the facts of how you've performed relative to metrics, as documented in your periodic reports. Do not characterize your work as "superlative" (or the like). Leave that part for your boss.

Include, as part of the package, the e-mail documenting the agreement you made with your boss in Step 1. That way your boss will be aware not only that you exceeded expectations but that you remember what was promised you.

4. USE "SURPRISES" TO EXTRACT CONCESSIONS.

With all the groundwork you've laid, your performance review will probably end up being a formality. You'll get a high rating, a pat on the back, and the reward you were promised.

However, even if you follow all the steps above, you may end up being blindsided. Examples:

- "I can't give you that raise because there's just been a salary freeze."
- "I can't send you to that trade convention in Hawaii because you didn't do [activity that's being mentioned now for the first time]."
- "Your promotion is on hold because [situation based on corporate politics]."

If you hadn't laid the groundwork, all you would be able to say at this point would be, "Oh. OK." However, since you *have* laid the groundwork, you've now got your boss in a position where the boss has reneged on a commitment, which means the boss *owes* you.

As calmly as possible, restate the fact that you've exceeded the boss's expectations and that the boss made a specific promise to you in the event that you did so. Then ask the boss what he or she *is* going to do, like so:

- "I understand that there's a salary freeze. How are you planning to get an exception in my case?"
- "Since this is the first time I've heard of this goal, I'm confused about how you expected me to fulfill it. So if you're not sending me to Hawaii, what *are* you going to do for me, since I exceeded the expectations that you set at the beginning of the year?"
- "That sounds like a tough problem. Since the promotion is now outside your control, what about things that are inside your control, like comp days? Rather than the promotion, how about an extra week off this year?"

Do *not* let your boss wriggle out of a commitment without you receiving some kind of concession in return. Otherwise your boss will always find a way to get out of any commitments that he or she makes.

At the end of the performance review, repeat the same conversation that you had in Step 1. Document the results of that conversation.

USING PERFORMANCE REVIEWS

- **FIND** out what you must accomplish and document the conversation.

- **TRACK** and report on your accomplishments against your metrics.

- **EITHER** write the performance review draft or provide "inputs" to same.

- **IF** the boss attempts to renege, insist on some other reward.

SECRET 5

How to Ask for a Raise

In the previous secret, I explained how to use your performance review to extract concessions from your boss. This secret works during your performance review but can also get you a raise even when it's not your review time. Here's how.

1. UNDERSTAND WHY COMPANIES GIVE RAISES.

Companies view your salary as an expense, so asking for a raise is asking your boss to spend more of the company's profit, cash reserves, or borrowed money on you, rather than on other priorities.

From the management perspective, your salary (and raise) has nothing whatsoever to do with what you need to stay alive or what you deserve to be paid. Both salaries and raises are based entirely on the cost of replacing you.

If the cost of replacing you is greater than what they're spending on your salary, you can ask for a raise and reasonably expect to get one. If not, you won't get the raise. It's really that simple.

2. KNOW YOUR POINTS OF LEVERAGE.

When you ask for a raise, you're asking your boss to compare the cost of giving you a raise with the cost of replacing you. It is therefore in your interest to increase your boss's awareness of that cost of replacement. Five costs come into play:

1. *Salary cost.* If you're being paid less than the average salary of somebody doing the same job you're doing, in the region where you are currently located, it's likely that your boss will need to offer a replacement more than you're being paid.

2. *Recruitment cost.* Finding candidates who have specific skills, interviewing them, and selecting a person (who may or may not accept) takes time and money. There will also be direct expenses if your boss needs to use a professional recruiter.

3. *Training cost.* If you have specialized skills and knowledge that are not generally available in the job candidate pool, your company will need to provide training in those skills and that knowledge to your replacement.

4. *Collateral damage cost.* If coworkers and customers see your presence as valuable, the company may lose (and therefore be forced to replace) coworkers and customers who leave as the result of your absence.

5. *Lost opportunity cost.* If you decide to leave for a better job, there will be a period of time when what you're doing isn't getting done. Depending on what you do, that can mean lost productivity or profit.

Please note that none of these costs have any meaning whatsoever unless you are actually prepared to leave your job. That's why you must always have other opportunities in the hopper. (See "Secret 22. How to Achieve Career Security.")

3. LAY THE GROUNDWORK.

Now that you know your leverage points, you can lay the groundwork for a productive discussion of your salary and why your company should be paying you more.

We'll start with the easiest element: salary ranges. Many websites contain salary ranges for job categories sorted for experience and geography.

If your job fits neatly into one of those categories and you're being paid less than the average salary and you're doing at least an average job, you obviously have a case for getting a raise. Unfortunately, it's not always that simple.

If you're an above-average worker, it becomes a judgment call (on the part of your boss) as to how much better you're doing compared to that average. So you'll need to show that you're exceptional (more on this later).

Similarly, if you've created your own unique job position (see "Secret 24. How to Find Your Dream Job") or have ended up doing more than one type of job (like both selling and providing technical support), the categories in the published salary ranges may not apply.

For example, at one point very early in my career I was responsible not only for writing computer operating manuals but also for designing the system we were using to create them. In this case the average salary for a technical writer wasn't a meaningful metric, because what I was doing was unique. (As it happens, I asked for and received double-digit annual salary increases for several years.)

However, if the categories *are* relevant, and it's clear you're being underpaid, e-mail your boss an FYI link to the sites. Rest assured, your boss will get the point.

Beyond that, many bosses aren't fully aware that it's probably going to be an expensive hassle to replace you, so you need to gather information that makes these costs more obvious.

Casually mention (long before you ask for the raise) that "HR professionals estimate it costs between two to three times an employee's annual salary to replace that employee." That your boss now knows this fact and knows *you* know, you have additional leverage.

Now make a list of all the training you've received, either through courses or on the job, since you were hired. Compose an e-mail like this to your boss:

```
Jill, I was thinking about all that I've learned
here (see list below) and wanted to thank you for
the investment that you and the company have made
in my career.
```

This e-mail is appropriate (you *are* grateful, right?) while also subtly surfacing how much it would cost to train somebody else.

Finally, solicit e-mails of praise from customers and coworkers when they feel you've done a good job. For example, suppose you get a thank-you phone call from a coworker in another department. Send the coworker the following response:

```
You're certainly welcome! Hey, would you mind
sending an e-mail to my boss saying how much I
helped you out? Don't forget to CC me!
```

Ideally, you want your boss to be getting an audit trail of kudos that not only document what a great job you're doing but subtly imply that customers and coworkers might be unhappy if you left to work elsewhere.

4. GATHER YOUR DOCUMENTATION.

Set up a meeting with your boss to "discuss your future." Before the meeting, create a list of the contributions you've made to the financial success of the company. The list should be the *results* of your activities, rather than a list of activities themselves.

WRONG:

- Worked with Acme proposal team.
- Handled customer information requests.

RIGHT:

- Contributed specifications to the Acme proposal that led to a $1 million sale.
- Improved our overall customer satisfaction figures by 25 percent.

Ideally you'll have kudo e-mails that support the list. For example, for the first item above, you might want an e-mail from the head of the proposal team praising your contribution and stating that it was crucial to getting the customer to buy.

Print two hard copies of the above. If the salary range information you've gathered on the Web is relevant, print two copies of that too. Highlight the relevant columns or rows. You are now ready to ask for your raise.

5. STATE YOUR CASE.

When your meeting begins, take the lead and set the tone by opening with: "I want to discuss what I see as a discrepancy between my value to the company and how I'm being compensated."

Your boss will not be overjoyed that you're bringing this subject up. However, if you've laid the groundwork (Step 3), he or she will certainly not be surprised. Your boss may try to cut off the conversation with something like:

- "We can't give you a raise right now."
- "We can only discuss raises at your performance review."
- "Corporate policy says no raises this year."

If so, you respond with, "Who said anything about a raise? I want to discuss the discrepancy between my value to the company and what I'm being paid."

Give your boss one copy of the material you've gathered and review it with him or her. Since you've laid the groundwork, there's a good chance that your boss will simply concede that you've got a point and there is a discrepancy. If so, jump to Step 7.

6. ANSWER ANY OBJECTIONS.

If your boss objects to your characterization of your contributions, neither argue nor concede the point. Instead respond in a way that agrees with what your boss is saying but reinforces your point:

Example 1:

> *Boss:* I don't think you had all that big an impact on the Acme proposal.

WRONG:

> *You:* I disagree, but whatever you say.

RIGHT:

> *You:* I can see how it might seem that way from your perspective. However, it's clear that I had an impact as evidenced by this e-mail from Acme's head of manufacturing.

Example 2:

> *Boss:* It cost a lot of money to train you. You should feel grateful.

WRONG:

> *You:* It was hard work learning all of that and I should be paid for that hard work.

RIGHT:

> *You:* Yes, I appreciate that the training has allowed me to make more of a contribution to the company and increase my value, which is why there's now a discrepancy.

Example 3:

> *Boss:* We expect this kind of excellence from everyone.

WRONG:

> *You:* Yeah, but I think I'm more excellent so you should pay me more.

RIGHT:

> *You:* I'm pleased that you realize that my performance has been excellent. I see it that way too.

Remember: your goal is to get the boss to concede that there is indeed a discrepancy between what you're being paid and what you're worth. After you've fielded any objections that your boss has raised, ask:

> *You:* Have we established that I should be paid more based upon my value to the company?

If the boss answers no, the discussion is over. You can conclude that you're not going to get a raise from this boss, regardless of what you say or do. That's bad news, but at least now you know.

If the boss answers yes or maybe (which in this case means "Yes, but I don't like where this conversation is headed"), move to the final step.

7. PUT THE BALL IN THE BOSS'S COURT AND KEEP IT THERE.

Once you've established that you should be paid more, ask the boss, "What do you intend to do?"

Either you will now get a commitment ("I'm giving you a ten percent raise") or the boss will make some attempt to stall or change the subject. No matter what he or she says, keep driving toward a commitment while you've got the advantage.

Example 1:

> *Boss:* I'll see what I can do.
> *You:* Exactly what are you going to do?

Example 2:

> *Boss:* I can't give you a raise because there's a salary freeze.
> *You:* We both know there are always exceptions. How are you going to get around the freeze so that I'm paid what I'm worth?

Example 3:

> *Boss:* I can get you a raise if you take on project XYZ.
> *You:* I'm happy to talk about future projects, but we've already established that I'm being paid less than I'm worth. What do you intend to do about that now?

Key point: once you've gotten your boss to admit that there's a discrepancy between your value to the company and what you're being paid, do not let your boss off the hook until you've gotten a commitment with a number attached to it.

ASKING FOR A RAISE

- **NOBODY** cares what you need, want, or expect to be paid.

- **YOUR** salary is dependent on your financial contribution.

- **LET** your boss know how much it would cost to replace you.

- **GATHER** information to buttress your case.

- **ESTABLISH** a discrepancy between your value and your pay.

- **FIELD** objections so they reinforce your case.

- **PUSH** until you've gotten a commitment with a number.

How to Handle Unreasonable Requests

Bosses (even great ones) can be unreasonable. You must therefore be prepared to react appropriately when the boss asks you to do things that either are outside your job description or would require too many extra hours of work.

1. DECIDE WHETHER THE REQUEST IS TRULY UNREASONABLE.

If you're salaried, by far the most common unreasonable request will be for you to regularly work more than forty hours a week. Also common are assignments that are "beneath" your job role as it's usually defined, such as being asked to do data entry when you've been hired to provide technical support.

Other unreasonable requests might involve providing various kinds of personal services to the boss. For example, I recently read of one manager who expected her employees to cater her private party.

Ultimately it's up to *you* to decide what's unreasonable *for you*. Remember, though, if you don't draw the line now, what was once an unreasonable request will become an implicit part of your general job description. And that will make it much harder to refuse similar requests in the future.

If you decide that the request is truly beyond the pale, skip directly to Step 3. If the request is in a bit of a gray area, proceed to Step 2. Special case: if your boss requests something that is actually illegal, contact your lawyer and activate your escape plan (see "Secret 22. How to Achieve Career Security").

2. RESTATE THE REQUEST AS A *QUID PRO QUO*.

If your boss has shown a willingness in the past to trade favor for favor, you may be able to use the unreasonable request to your advantage. For example, if your boss has previously rewarded extra hours of work with under-the-table time off, maybe you can make a deal.

If you think you can, estimate the amount of time and effort your boss is requesting. Based on that estimate, come up with something comparable that will advance your own career or enhance your own life. Example: "I'd be happy to cater your party if you'll send me to the user group conference in Tahiti this winter."

What's important here is that you're establishing a precedent. By demanding something substantial in return, you're making it clear to the boss that you're no chump. This will minimize unreasonable requests in the future.

3. IF NECESSARY, JUST SAY NO.

There is a right way and a wrong way to do this.

The wrong way is to make excuses. Example: "I'd love to work this weekend but I'd risk being arrested for child neglect." While this seems like an easy way out, it allows the unreasonable request to pop up later in a slightly different form. (For example: "How about working through your lunch hours?")

A better way to say no is to force a discussion of priorities that puts the unreasonable request into perspective. Say something like, "If I do A thoroughly, I won't be able to do B thoroughly. Which of the two is the real priority?"

If the boss persists, you may need to be more direct, like "No, I don't intend to do that because [reason that makes sense to you and hopefully to the boss as well]." Here's an example from very early in my career:

> *Boss:* Please type up this handwritten memo for me.
> *Me:* I was hired as a writer, not as a typist, so I'm not going to be able to do that for you.

This approach could be perceived as the "wrong attitude" and result in the boss's getting annoyed and possibly putting you at future disadvantage. That's why you've got to have your options open.

While being this direct with your boss may seem difficult, saying no is like any other skill. It gets easier the more you do it.

SHORTCUT

NEGOTIATING UNREASONABLE REQUESTS

- **BE** flexible about what's unreasonable.
- **IF** you agree, get something in return.
- **CULTIVATE** the courage to say no.

7

How to Cope with a Bully

Some bosses can't keep their temper, and yell at their employees. If your boss tries this management "technique," you need to nip the situation in the bud. If you don't, the behavior will recur and you'll find yourself dreading every day at work.

1. REALIZE THAT THIS IS ABNORMAL BEHAVIOR.

When bosses yell at employees, some employees assume that this is normal, if unpleasant, boss behavior. It's not. Regardless of the business situation, regardless of how tense the boss becomes, you have the right to be treated with civility and respect.

Bosses who vent anger and frustration on others in the workplace are being childish and self-indulgent. They are using other people as punching bags to calm their own fears and worries. Bullying is *abusive*.

2. DO NOT PLACATE.

For many people, the first response when confronted with an angry boss is to stare aghast and then try to get the boss to calm down by apologizing—even if there's no good reason the employee should be apologizing.

Unfortunately, any attempt to placate somebody who is acting this way communicates that you consider the behavior acceptable and you're willing to tolerate it. Instead, do the following:

3. RAISE YOUR OWN INTENSITY LEVEL.

Bullies, like dogs, can smell fear. And, like dogs, they tend to back off when the other dog snarls back. Do not yell because that will escalate the conflict. Instead, match the intensity in the other person's face and eyes.

Think of it this way: what everybody (including your boss) wants is a connection—a sense that he or she is being heard. However, you can't really connect with a boss if you're wimping out. So glare back and prepare to put some steel in your voice.

4. CALL THE BULLY'S BLUFF.

State that you're willing to help resolve the problem that's got the bully upset, but that you won't tolerate abuse. Don't mince words. Make it clear that you expect everyone around you, including your boss, to behave toward you in a civilized manner.

Watch for the reaction. Nine times out of ten your boss will back down, because when reasonable people lose their tempers, they know that they're behaving poorly and welcome the opportunity to recover their poise.

5. IF THE ABUSE CONTINUES, WALK AWAY.

Sometimes, though, the bully will be so carried away by negative emotions that he or she won't be able to stop. If so, state that you'll be glad to discuss the matter once the bully is willing to treat you with the respect that you deserve.

Then leave the immediate area or, if you're on the phone, hang up. By doing so you are not only preventing abuse, you're teaching the bully a lesson and saving the bully from further damaging his or her dignity.

6. DISTANCE YOURSELF FROM THE SITUATION.

If the bully does not back down and you are forced to walk away or hang up, you'll undoubtedly be either upset or angry yourself. If at all possible, do not interact with the other people with whom you work, lest you say something you'll regret.

Instead, go somewhere private and cope with your emotions in whatever way works for you. You may want to call a friend or family member to vent your frustration and get some moral support.

7. AFTER THE BULLY CALMS DOWN, DISCUSS THE ISSUE.

Once you've demanded, and gotten, civil behavior—then and only then—address whatever problem has made the person so upset. When you start the conversation with the (now hopefully calmer) boss, explain that you are committed to resolving the issue.

Be positive and be professional. Yes, it's a shame that your boss lacks emotional strength and self-awareness, but the purpose of the conversation is to address a business issue, not to make the boss feel bad for acting like a jerk.

8. REASSESS THE RELATIONSHIP.

Now comes the difficult part. Ask yourself, "Was this a one-time event or is this something that happens all the time?" If the event was unusual, let it slide. People are human. Sometimes they lose it.

However, if this kind of crap is habitual, it's time to activate your escape plan (see "Secret 22. How to Achieve Career Security").

DEALING WITH A BULLY

▓ **DON'T** try to calm the bully down or apologize.

▓ **INSIST** on respectful, professional behavior.

▓ **IF** the unprofessional behavior continues, leave the immediate area.

▓ **COPE** with your own emotions privately.

▓ **REVISIT** the issue at a later date.

▓ **DECIDE** whether the relationship is worth it.

PART **II**

How to Manage
Your Coworkers

Your relationship with your coworkers is almost as important as your relationship with your boss. After all, you see them more often than your boss, you need them in order to get your own job done, and their day-to-day behavior is a huge part of your work experience.

Just as you must manage your relationship with your boss, you must also manage the relationships you have with your coworkers. You want them to help you become more successful while you do the same for them.

This part of the book helps you understand your coworkers better so you can work together to achieve mutual goals. It also helps you know what to do with coworkers who are not, well, all that helpful.

This part of the book is organized as follows:

■ "How to Earn Respect from Your Peers" explains what you can and should do regularly to ensure that your coworkers think of you as a valuable contributor and important part of their team.

■ "How to Play Clean Office Politics" provides a simple model for interacting with coworkers so they help you out and you help them out. The emphasis here is on making the kind of deals that help everyone become more successful.

■ "How to Recruit a Mentor" gives guidance for finding a coworker (usually not your boss) who will take a personal interest in your career and help you navigate the complexities of your job.

■ "The Ten Types of Annoying Coworker" describes people you'll probably run into sooner or later and how to deal with their odd (and often amusing) behavior patterns.

■ "How to Handle Corporate Lawyers" deals with the special case of working with lawyers, who have a habit of "gumming up" the smooth flow of business. I explain how to use them effectively, rather than let them become roadblocks.

■ "How to Use Social Media" explains how to position yourself online so your coworkers (and everyone else you work with) understand who you are and what you're trying to accomplish.

■ "How to Shine in a Meeting" teaches you how to avoid meetings that are useless to your career and how to look good in those meetings that you either elect to attend or simply must attend.

8

How to Earn Respect from Your Peers

Contrary to popular belief, you can't get respect from a job title or a position on an organizational chart. There are six ways to earn respect, regardless of the organization you're in or the role you've been hired to fill:

1. BE YOURSELF, NOT YOUR ROLE.

Sometimes people think they must create a persona in order to command the respect of others. Bosses think they should be authority figures, salespeople think they should be fast talkers, engineers think they should be nerds, and so forth.

However, who you *really* are is more likely to command respect than your ability to play a role that's unnatural to you. People have a natural ability to detect fakery, and see fakers as untrustworthy, insecure, and ultimately insignificant.

On the other hand, people are drawn to individuals who truly *are* what they seem to be. Being yourself (and at your best for whoever you are) is therefore the foundation of earning respect.

2. SHOW CURIOSITY ABOUT OTHER PEOPLE.

If you're curious about other people, you listen, truly listen, to what they have to say. When people realize that they're really being heard, they'll tell you what's important (to them) about their jobs, their dreams, their fears, their goals.

That knowledge not only gives you perspective on how to do your job better, but also helps you see how you can best help others. That's essential, because whenever you help other people, it increases their respect for you.

In a larger sense, curiosity about other people helps you do just about any job better. Bosses more easily manage people when they understand them, salespeople more easily discover customer needs, and engineers even build products that more people want to use.

3. GIVE CREDIT WHERE DUE.

There are times (such as when you're updating your social media profile) when you'll want to toot your own horn. However, if you want your coworkers to respect you, you'll make those times few and far between.

In business, almost every accomplishment is a team effort. When you publicly praise the people who helped you get your job done, they (and everyone else) will be far more likely to help you next time around.

More important, giving credit where it's due shows respect for others, which in turn creates more respect for you.

4. DRESS APPROPRIATELY FOR THE JOB.

Rightly or wrongly, people judge based on the visual signals you provide to them. When you meet people for the first time, they take in everything about you: your clothes, watch, jewelry, briefcase, makeup, muscle tone, facial expression, and so forth.

It is therefore in your interest to think about how the overall "package" is likely to seem to the other person. Consciously create a set of visual signals that is likely to communicate that you're a person with whom the other person would want to do business.

If you're not naturally style-conscious, the best way to hone your appearance is to get feedback from a colleague or perhaps your boss. If there's a problem, make adjustments until you're presenting a visual image that matches your ambition.

Does this mean that you might have to spend money buying expensive clothes? Absolutely, if the nature of the job demands it. If you can't afford "the look," make getting the right clothes your top financial priority.

5. THINK BEFORE YOU SPEAK.

Nobody respects motormouths or blabbermouths. Therefore, whenever you intend to say something, take a moment to frame your thoughts and decide how best to communicate them.

Pausing before you speak not only keeps you from half-articulating half-baked ideas, it also makes you seem thoughtful and more wise. And if you're responding to somebody's comments, it shows you've taken the time to digest what you've heard.

Thinking before speaking also prevents you from spreading gossip and saying things that you'll later regret. As Abraham Lincoln said, "Better to remain silent and be thought a fool than to speak out and remove all doubt."

6. ARTICULATE WITH AUTHORITY.

When people get nervous, their voices tend to move upward so the sound emerges from the nose, which turns even deep wisdom into an irritating whine. Speaking from your chest makes you sound (and feel) more confident and therefore worthy of respect.

Similarly, mid-sentence verbal tics ("uhhh...," "you know...,"

"I mean...," etc.) and a questioning uptick at the end of a sentence make you sound unsure and vague. People will respect you more if you sound as if you know what you're talking about.

Sometimes bad verbal habits are so ingrained that the speaker doesn't even notice them. Record yourself and listen to how you really sound. Practice until you sound confident, both to yourself and to others.

SHORTCUT

EARNING RESPECT FROM COWORKERS

- ■ **BE** yourself rather than your role.

- ■ **SHOW** interest in other people.

- ■ **ALWAYS** share the limelight.

- ■ **DRESS** and groom to match your ambitions.

- ■ **PAUSE** before speaking to mentally frame your thoughts.

- ■ **SPEAK** from your chest without verbal tics or end-of-sentence rises in pitch.

How to Play Clean Office Politics

Most people think office politics are bad for business. Nothing could be further from the truth. Office politics are an integral part of getting things done, whether you're the CEO, a salesperson, or an intern hired for the summer.

The word *politics* comes from the Greek *politikos*, which means "of, for, or relating to citizens." Far from being something negative, politics are nothing less than the art and science of influencing people.

Below is a four-step approach to office politics that doesn't resort to tricks or deception (aka dirty politics, which *are* bad for business as described in "Secret 43. How to Thwart Dirty Office Politics"):

1. UNCOVER AND UNDERSTAND NEEDS.

Playing politics consists of balancing the needs of multiple people so they can come together to make a decision. In business, people have four general types of needs:

1. *Personal needs* reflect the personality of the individual and what that individual expects and wants out of an experience, such as recognition, compensation, challenge, amusement, and so forth.

2. *Career needs* consist of the individual's plans to achieve those personal needs by moving through different jobs and companies. Career needs emerge from personal needs. For example, a need to be in the limelight is a personal need; the need to become a lead programmer (in order to be in the limelight) is a career need.

3. *Job needs* consist of the resources individuals require to advance their career needs and personal needs. For example, in order for the title of "lead programmer" to be meaningful, there must be a staff of programmers to lead.

4. *Organizational needs* are the total job needs of the individuals within a group. For example, in order for there to be a lead programmer and a staff of programmers to lead, the organization might need a new computer and new software for the programmers to program upon.

Once you understand your own needs (on various levels) and the needs of those you work with, you're ready to play politics.

2. BUILD ALLIANCES.

Office politics consist of making deals to support the satisfying of another's needs in return for that person's support in the satisfying of your needs.

For example, if you've got a colleague who wants to be head programmer and you want to be manager of quality control, you might tell the colleague: "I'll support your bid to become head programmer if you'll support my bid to become manager of quality control."

The keys to making such alliances work are thus (1) figuring out what you want, (2) figuring out what the other person wants, and (3) agreeing to get there together.

Take care when building alliances. As a general rule, you want to work with people who can be trusted both to hold up their side of the deal and to do the right thing by the rest of the firm.

For example, you probably don't want to make a deal that involves promoting a complete idiot to be Chief Technical Officer—at least, not if you want your firm to succeed.

However, if, all things considered, it really doesn't matter all that much whether Jack or Jill gets the promotion, it's OK to support Jill if she's the one who's more willing and able to reciprocate the favor. (And, of course, so much the better if you're certain that Jill is the better choice.)

3. TRACK FAVORS AND OBLIGATIONS.

In addition to alliances, politics consist of a less formal trading of favors. Again, it's a simple concept: you do a favor for somebody and then, at a later date, you get to "call in" the favor by asking that person to do something for you. And vice versa, naturally.

Playing office politics therefore requires that you keep close track of whom you owe and about how much, and who owes you and about how much.

Knowing the first keeps you from being blindsided by unexpected requests. Knowing the second allows you to assess whether or not you've got the political power to achieve your goal, if politics are needed to achieve it.

It need hardly be said that trading favors is a great way to strengthen your alliances.

Some negotiation is usually involved in assessing the value of past favors versus the value of future favors. Be aware that everyone has his or her own mental tally, which might not agree 100 percent with yours.

4. LINE UP YOUR DUCKS.

All this effort comes to fruition at decision-making time. Your goal is to make certain (as far as possible) that everybody is supporting the decision you prefer, by making your alliances and indulging in favor-trading.

For example, suppose your firm has a choice between two software vendors. Your research tells you Vendor A is the right choice, but you're aware that some of the misguided dunderheads you work with believe that Vendor B is a better option.

When the big meeting takes place to decide which vendor to hire, you want as many people as possible at the conference room table predisposed to agree with you that the company should go with Vendor A. You therefore use politics to fill the meeting with your dependable allies.

Similarly, suppose you want a promotion but there's another candidate vying for it. This is an excellent time to call in your markers and have your allies heap praise upon you and insist you'd be perfect for the job.

SHORTCUT

USING POLITICS TO GET THINGS DONE

- **FIND** out what other people need and want.
- **BUILD** mutually useful alliances with those you can trust.
- **KEEP** track of the favors you owe and the ones owed you.
- **USE** your alliances at key points to help achieve your goals.

10

How to Recruit a Mentor

A mentor is a coworker or colleague, usually older and hopefully wiser, who takes a personal interest in you, provides advice and guidance, and uses his or her connections to help move your career forward.

1. UNDERSTAND THE RELATIONSHIP.

Misconceptions surround mentoring (and being mentored), which makes it easy to think mentoring is a bigger deal than it actually is.

On the one hand, popular culture encourages gooey romanticism connected with the idea of a zen master taking a young novice under his wing. (Think Yoda and Luke Skywalker.)

On the other hand, you've got companies that launch "mentoring programs" that are integrated into their official employee orientation, as if there were some way to formalize a relationship that, by its very nature, is informal.

The reality lies somewhere in between. Chances are that as you proceed in your career, you'll have a number of relationships in which another person agrees to spend his or her time and energy helping you.

Your mentors won't be Yoda, but (if you're lucky) they'll be more than just some old fart whom HR assigned to be your mentor because it decided he needed something extra to do with his time.

It's pretty obvious what you're getting out of the mentoring relationship: access to experience, perspective, and contacts. What the mentor gets out of it is a little more complex.

Some mentors have a strong need to teach, some crave the gratitude, and others may simply want somebody in the organization who they know will watch their backs. As you work with your mentor, you'll figure out what's wanted in return.

2. KNOW WHAT YOU LACK.

The first step to finding a mentor is realizing that you've got a hole in your experience that you can't plug by reading a book or taking a seminar.

Suppose you're a natural at programming but weak at understanding people. If your goal is to be an engineering manager, you'll need to know how to handle personnel issues. That's hard to learn from a book but easier if somebody coaches you.

In my personal case, it was the other way around. I always understood people fairly well, but when I started out in high tech, I lacked any useful technical skills. That led to my first mentor, who taught me the basics of programming and system design.

You do not need to work in the same building, or even the same company, as your mentor. I've mentored (and been mentored by) people I've never met in person, but with whom I frequently traded e-mails and phone calls.

3. ASK FOR ADVICE, NOT TO BE MENTORED.

Asking for advice is a compliment to whomever you ask, and most people enjoy teaching what they've learned. However, asking somebody to be your mentor is just plain creepy. It's like asking somebody to marry you after you've just met.

Mentorships develop over time. Mentors find that they enjoy providing advice and guidance and continue to make themselves available. Those being mentored find they enjoy getting advice and express gratitude for it.

There's no specific point at which the relationship changes from one of simply giving and receiving advice to something ongoing.

4. BE KIND WHEN YOU OUTGROW IT.

There will come a time when you no longer need the advice and guidance of your mentor. When that happens the relationship must change, which can be painful for the mentor.

As any parent who has raised children to adulthood knows, it's bittersweet when your children no longer need you. The same thing is true of mentors. Therefore, when you've outgrown the relationship, don't just dump your mentor.

Get some distance but keep the connection going. Hopefully what started as a mentoring relationship will develop into a friendship between equals.

SHORTCUT

RECRUITING A MENTOR

- **MENTORS** crave to teach people what they've learned.
- **SEEK** out mentors who have experience and skills you lack.
- **ASK** for advice and let the relationship develop.
- **BE** kind when you outgrow the relationship.

The Ten Types of Annoying Coworker

Most of the time, getting along with coworkers is simply a matter of being a reasonably nice person and minding your own business. However, there are ten types of coworker who can be real hassles. Here's how to deal with them:

1. THE WAFFLER

Because they're afraid that they might get blamed for making a bad decision, wafflers study everything to death, always seeking a mythical single last bit of information that will make everything clear.

Wafflers hope to avoid a decision until circumstances make that decision unnecessary. If the indecision creates failure through inaction, the waffler becomes indignant when held responsible. "It's not MY fault!"

If your job or project hinges on a decision that's in the hands of a waffler, your best move is to make the decision in such a way that he thinks he's made it himself. Establish a deadline for the decision, with a default if no course of action is chosen.

Example: "Since I need a decision on this by [date], if I do not hear from you by then, I will proceed as if the decision is..."

2. THE CONQUEROR

There's nothing wrong with being competitive. However, there are some people who are so competitive that they start losing perspective, so beating the other guy becomes more important than doing the right thing.

For example, suppose you have two highly competitive salespeople working for firms that are normally in competition but that now must work together to develop a huge sales opportunity that could benefit both firms.

Because the two salespeople see each other as competitors, they'll likely spend more time jockeying for control of the account and trying to squeeze each other out than actually developing the opportunity.

To deal with a conqueror, channel that competitiveness into helping an entire team to win, rather than just the conqueror. Be forewarned, though: no matter what, the conqueror will hog the limelight after the win.

3. THE DRAMATIST

Dramatists (aka drama queens) turn almost everything into hissy fits, replete with dollops of pique and umbrage. They seem to draw energy from the drama they create even though everyone else finds the drama to be draining.

Dramatists, above all, crave being the *center of attention*. Like a ham actor on a sound stage, they exaggerate their expressions, make broad gestures, offend others, and feign outrage, all in a desperate attempt to say, "Look at me! I'm important!"

Unfortunately, giving in to dramatists only increases, rather than decreases, their appetite for attention. Your best bet with dramatists is to ignore their histrionics until they run out of steam.

No matter what the dramatist says, do not react. When the histrionics are over, casually acknowledge that the dramatist has expressed an opinion, then move on to whatever issue actually needs to be addressed.

4. THE ICONOCLAST

Iconoclasts thrive on the negative attention that comes from disrespecting other people, especially those in authority. They'll break even the most sensible rules (social and business alike), just to show they can get away with it.

For example, I once worked with a guy who couldn't resist describing our boss to everyone (including many people who knew the boss socially) as "shit for brains."

Admittedly, our boss wasn't exactly a klieg light. Even so, the constant negativity made a bad situation worse, except for my coworker, who clearly enjoyed the attention that came from verbally bucking authority.

The best way to deal with iconoclasts is to distance yourself from them while you're at work. While they're sometimes entertaining, iconoclasts eventually get axed, along with anybody who's seen as part of their clique.

5. THE DRONER

Droners are always ready to give a presentation—usually one that everyone has heard before. They list their bullet points on multiple slides and with grim determination read each one aloud.

The problem with droners is that, most of the time, they don't realize that they're boring. They may truly believe their data-rich slides are fascinating, or at least so vitally important that they deserve your full attention.

The best way to cope with droners is to try to avoid meetings to which they have been invited. If that's not possible, find a way to make the drone time useful. For example, you might answer e-mails on your tablet under the guise of taking notes.

If you can control the rules of the meeting, you can set a "one slide per person" rule for meeting, or better yet a "no PowerPoint" rule. You'll be surprised how much this will force even a droner to focus on what's really important.

6. THE FRENEMY

A frenemy pretends to be your biggest cheerleader, your best confidant, and the only person who's really on your side. Meanwhile the frenemy is subtly sabotaging everything you do.

Under the guise of praise, a frenemy will make a comment that's intended to sap your self-confidence. Example: "You did so well at that big presentation that almost nobody noticed the typos."

A frenemy is always ready to help you out with a problem, in theory at least. When it comes to actually delivering the goods, the frenemy always has a plausible excuse as to why it just wasn't possible.

To cope with frenemies, either avoid them completely or, if that's not possible, be polite but do nothing to encourage the "friendship." The frenemy's power lies in the ability to get under your skin. That's more difficult if you keep your distance.

7. THE TOADY

In business everyone sucks up to the boss, at least some of the time. It's human nature to ingratiate yourself with those in power, and even the best bosses expect and appreciate the occasional word of homage.

However, there's a huge difference between giving your boss the occasional kiss on the butt and permanently wedging your face in the crack. Toadies constantly praise everything the boss does, hoping to receive favors in return.

Toadies are bad coworkers for two reasons. First, they waste their time and energy stroking the boss's ego rather than doing productive work. Second, bosses who tolerate toadyism become impervious to any advice that's not fulsome praise.

If you end up working with toadies, understand that the real problem is the boss. Therefore you have exactly two choices: find another boss or become a toady yourself.

8. THE VAMPIRE

Workplace vampires suck all the energy out of the room the moment they appear. Vampires always have a reason something won't work, a story that illustrates the futility of trying, and an endless list of unsolvable problems.

Vampires aren't depressed. Far from it. They obtain a great deal of pleasure from squishing the positive feelings of those around them. The only time they really smile is after they've propelled everybody else into a sulk.

Traditional vampires shrivel and die when they're exposed to sunlight. Workplace vampires react similarly when exposed to sweet reason. Say stuff like, "Wow, that's a pretty negative spin." Then move on as if the negative comment hadn't been made.

As long as you refuse to get caught up in the vampire's negative miasma, the vampire will get frustrated and decamp to some other meeting, or some other poor sap's office, in order to continue sucking energy.

9. THE PARASITE

Parasites wait to see what ideas become popular inside a firm and then, when it's clear an idea has support and traction, position themselves as its sponsor and (by implication) the brains behind it.

This behavior (aka "finding a parade and getting out in front of it") is extremely common in large organizations. The reason is simple: being a parasite entails far less risk than being an entrepreneur.

To thwart parasites, call them on their behavior the minute they try to get out in front of the parade. Say something like, "Since you're completely new to the project, you might want to hold back a little until you understand what's going on."

Beyond that, always keep an "audit trail" of your contributions to a project in the form of regular status reports. Send them to the parasite's manager if the parasite continues to attempt to steal credit.

10. THE GENIUS

Geniuses are legends in their own minds. They talk and talk about the amazing stuff they've done in the past and their equally amazing plans for the future. Somehow they never seem to do anything in the here and now.

Geniuses take on projects but fail to follow through. As deadlines approach they can't be found. When the work is finally turned in (often by others who have covered for them), a genius will disappear for a while to "recuperate."

Dealing with geniuses requires persistence. Document what they're supposed to complete and lay out frequent milestones that the genius must meet in order for the project to be completed.

For example, suppose the genius is supposed to update the technical specifications for your sales proposal. Rather than waiting until the last minute to remind the genius it's due, send daily reminders of the commitment to both the genius and the genius's boss.

If this seems as if you're being a pest, it's because you *are* being a pest. Unfortunately, pestering geniuses is the only way to hold their feet to the fire.

THE TEN TYPES OF ANNOYING COWORKER

- **WAFFLERS** can't decide so force the issue.
- **CONQUERORS** must win so make them team leader.
- **DRAMATISTS** crave attention so ignore them.
- **ICONOCLASTS** break rules needlessly so avoid them.
- **DRONERS** are boring so find something else to do.
- **FRENEMIES** sabotage so keep them at arm's length.
- **TOADIES** mean you must either leave or become a toady yourself.
- **VAMPIRES** leech energy unless you stay upbeat.
- **PARASITES** steal credit so track who's contributed.
- **GENIUSES** are all talk, so pester them until they deliver.

12

How to Handle
Corporate Lawyers

Few things can gum up a business deal or put a damper on a great idea like the presence of an overzealous corporate lawyer. Fortunately corporate lawyers are relatively easy to handle. Here's how:

1. FLY BELOW THE RADAR.

Assuming you actually want to get things done, it's generally in your interest to keep lawyers out of the picture, unless your industry is one in which nothing gets done without them.

If you trust the people you're working with, conduct the majority of your business using simple, self-created contracts. These take the form of simple statements like "You will do A" and "I will do B."

Needless to say, flying below the radar means that you're taking on the risk yourself should something go wrong. If that *really* bothers you, then go ahead and get lawyers involved. However, remember that there's a price to pay, and it's not just the lawyer's fees.

2. ASK FOR AN OPINION, NOT APPROVAL.

Corporate lawyers are natural pessimists. It's their job to manage risks and to make certain that if something (like a contract dispute) goes to court, you and your company don't end up on the losing end.

The easiest way for a lawyer to eliminate risk is to make sure nothing happens—at all. That's why if you ask a corporate lawyer, "Should we do this unusual or unprecedented thing?" the answer will usually be no, regardless of whether it's a good idea or not.

Once you realize this, you're free to decide whether the risks (which the lawyer will definitely identify) are worth the benefits of going ahead anyway. You can also solicit suggestions for limiting those risks.

3. DON'T SETTLE FOR GIBBERISH.

Lawyers, like all experts, have a tendency to speak and write using jargon that's specific to their profession. In the case of lawyers, this habit is worse because they tend to see language as a way to create wiggle room rather than to communicate clearly.

In some situations (as when drawing up a complicated contract) it may be in your interest to let your lawyer play that game. However, when you're on the receiving end of this tactic, insist on clarifying these intentional ambiguities.

To do this, read each paragraph aloud to the lawyer and ask, "What does this mean in plain English?" When the lawyer responds, scratch out the legalese and write down what the lawyer just said.

4. GIVE LAWYERS PLENTY OF TIME.

Corporate lawyers don't benefit if a deal goes through, but they *do* get blamed if the deal turns into a debacle. Delay, to a corporate lawyer, is a good thing, because delay prevents bad things from happening.

Asking a corporate lawyer to do something quickly is like pushing a mule. The harder you push, the slower the mule moves. It's wiser to lay out a schedule and ask the lawyer if it's possible to get the work done by then.

If the situation involves opposing lawyers (e.g., your corporate lawyers are negotiating with your client's corporate lawyers), your best approach is to hunker down for a long wait.

5. CULTIVATE A RELATIONSHIP.

Contrary to popular opinion, lawyers are human beings and, as with all human beings, more likely to help those they know and like rather than those they don't know or actively dislike.

Therefore, if your firm has corporate lawyers, cultivate some kind of relationship with them ahead of time—long before you get into the situation where you need them to move quickly on your behalf.

Developing a relationship with corporate lawyers is just like developing one with anyone else at work. Ask about their jobs and backgrounds. Cultivate common interests.

Ideally you want lawyers to see you as you are: a person trying to get a job done, rather than a nuisance who wants them to commit to the unnatural act of approving an exceptional case quickly.

SHORTCUT

CORPORATE LAWYERS

- **WHENEVER** the risk is minimal, leave lawyers out of the loop.

- **LAWYERS** are not managers; get their advice but make your own decision.

- **INSIST** that legal gibberish be simplified into plain language.

- **NEVER** rush a lawyer because it will result in even more delay.

- **IF** you've got a corporate legal group, find somebody in it to befriend.

How to Use Social Media

Companies create brands because brands help buyers remember the experience they've had (or expect to have) with a company's products. A brand consists of three major elements: a brand name, a brand logo, and a corporate history.

For example, the Coca-Cola Company has several brand names (the most famous being Coke), a distinctive logo that the company infrequently changes, and a well-established history as a provider of tasty soft drinks for over a hundred years.

Similarly, you (as an individual) have a brand consisting of elements in the social media in which you participate: your name (brand name), your photo (brand logo), and your profile information (corporate history).

Here's how to use social media to brand yourself:

1. UNDERSTAND THE REWARDS AND RISKS.

Social media sites are fundamentally different from other forms of business communication. Conversations, voice mails, e-mails, and presentations are *narrowcast media*, meaning they are either one-to-one or one-to-few.

Social networking, on the other hand, is broadcast media on steroids, which means it is one-to-many-to-many-to-many. While you can limit access to your profiles on some sites, these sites are intended to be seen by all and sundry. Because of this they can have an outsize effect on your career, for good or bad.

Social networking is your primary vehicle for creating your brand and expanding awareness of it. However, like a corporation, you must protect your brand from becoming tarnished even as you work to establish it.

2. CREATE AN APPROPRIATE BRAND IMAGE.

Since your photo is your brand logo, you want a profile photo—the same on all sites—that reinforces your brand in a way that helps rather than hinders your career. If you can afford it, hire a professional photographer to shoot publicity photos. No selfies.

Meanwhile, try to expunge any online evidence of behavior that runs contrary to the image you're trying to create. Scrub your old social networking pages; if your friends have posted stuff you'd prefer not be seen, ask them to delete it.

Even unusual hobbies can throw employers and customers off, if you're not well known enough in your own field to make such details irrelevant. Despite the pressure to meld your business and personal lives, I recommend keeping your private life private.

Sometimes it's not possible to scrub something questionable from your past. For example, if you're arrested, your name and face can end up on a mug shot website and remain there even if you're not charged. If so, you'll need to change your name.

Another element of brand image is your literacy or lack of same. Spelling and grammatical errors in your profile will make people think that you're either stupid or careless, or both. If you're not a strong writer, hire a copy editor to go over your profile.

3. MAKE YOUR RÉSUMÉ RELEVANT.

For work purposes, the most important social media sites are the ones, such as LinkedIn, where you post your résumé. Most people make the dumb mistake of using that forum to post a generalized version of their employment history.

Why is that dumb? Because your online résumé is useful for only two things: positioning you for a new job, or strengthening your ability to do your current job. A generalized résumé accomplishes neither of these tasks.

If you are job hunting, you want your résumé to reflect whatever job you are currently pursuing. (I discuss this issue elsewhere in "Secret 25. How to Land a Job Interview.") Therefore, during a job hunt, you must constantly tweak your résumé to match your efforts.

If you are currently employed and not looking for another job, you want the people you work with (or sell to or buy from) to see you as qualified and authoritative in your current job. Therefore, scrub everything that's irrelevant to your current job.

In your résumé, describe only actions that you personally took, along with the specific, quantifiable effects of those actions. For example, if you work in public relations, nobody cares if your job title was "communications director." However, they might very well take notice if you got your CEO on CNN and the stock rose by 10 percent.

4. GET REALISTIC RECOMMENDATIONS.

Finally, LinkedIn allows other people to post recommendations. The problem with these endorsements is that everyone suspects you've simply queued up your best pals to be sock puppets that say nice things.

Nevertheless, it doesn't hurt to get some recommendations, but you want them to be realistic and believable, which means that they can't attempt to paint you as the most wonderful person in the world.

Ideally you want recommendations that reinforce the relevance of your résumé. Therefore, you may want to change or switch them, depending on whether you're job hunting or not, or on the type of job you're pursuing.

5. DON'T BLOG UNLESS YOU'RE A NATURAL.

Almost everybody who starts blogging gives up after a few weeks, after which the posts become few and far between, and eventually peter out altogether. What remains is an out-of-date blog that's a testament to your inability to blog regularly.

Blogging with substantial content is easy when you start (because everyone has something to say) but gets more difficult over time. I say this as a professional blogger who (as of this writing) has posted content every business day since February 2007.

If you're determined to blog, be realistic rather than ambitious. If you think you can post once a week, set a schedule to post every two weeks or every month. That way you're less likely to run out of things to say.

Microblogging (as on Twitter) is less of an issue because there's no need to constantly create anything of substance. In this case you're generally alerting people to content they might find useful or interesting, rather than creating it yourself.

Finally, don't expect your blog to generate lots of traffic. Very few blogs acquire a significant number of readers. Most of the time, the value of the blog is in providing more detail—about who you are and how you think—to people who are already interested in you.

6. SET RULES FOR YOUR ONLINE COMMENTING.

Because a poorly placed remark or off-color joke by an employee can damage a company's brand image, most big firms have very specific guidelines for what employees can and can't write online.

The same is true for your brand image. You are not doing yourself any favors by getting your brand name associated with discussions of anything that's irrelevant to your career. That's especially true if the discussions are political, religious, or sexual in nature.

If you feel that you simply *must* comment on such forums, use a pseudonym, not your brand name, and be aware that even then you might still be outed. Many careers have been ruined this way.

SHORTCUT

SOCIAL MEDIA

- **YOUR** personal brand will define how people see you.
- **GET** a professional portrait and expunge unprofessional photos.
- **CUSTOMIZE** your résumé to match your career goals.
- **SOLICIT** recommendations that are realistic and relevant.
- **AVOID** blogging unless you're being paid to do so.
- **KEEP** your irrelevant opinions off the Internet.

14

How to Shine in a Meeting

Business meetings have never been more popular. About 25 million meetings take place *every day* in corporate America alone. Conservatively, at least half of that time is wasted by aimless presentations and pointless discussions.

Because of this, attend business meetings sparingly and only if it advances your own agenda. Remember: if you spend only ninety minutes a day (on average) in meetings, by the time you're sixty-five they will have consumed *eight years* of your working life.

In "Secret 18. How to Hold a Productive Meeting," I explain how to make your own meetings go smoothly. In this secret I explain how to attend only those meetings that are useful, and how to work your own agenda into the meetings you do attend.

1. KNOW YOUR OWN AGENDA.

A business meeting consumes time, and since you have a limited amount of time, you want to attend only those business meetings that move you closer to your goals. This is impossible if you don't know what you're trying to accomplish.

If you do decide to attend a business meeting, you want the actions you take during the meeting to move you closer to your goals. Once again, impossible if you don't know what you're trying to accomplish.

Therefore, whenever you are confronted with the opportunity to attend a meeting, you should first review your personal and career goals so you can assess whether it will be time well spent, and how you'll spend the time if you attend.

2. KNOW WHY THE MEETING WAS CALLED.

Your strategy for dealing with a meeting varies according to the type of meeting. People call meetings for seven reasons:

1. *To get you to decide something.* The meeting caller wants to persuade or convince you to make a decision.

2. *To hone their own ideas.* The meeting caller wants the benefit of your experience and creativity on his or her own project.

3. *To convey information.* The meeting caller has information that he or she wants to communicate, but is too lazy to create a stand-alone document.

4. *To test out a presentation.* The meeting caller wants to rehearse a presentation in front of a live audience.

5. *To accomplish group writing.* The meeting caller intends to use the creation of a document to drive toward a consensus decision.

6. *To prove their own importance.* The meeting caller is establishing his or her place in the pecking order by wasting other people's time.

7. *To fulfill a process step.* The meeting caller is fulfilling a commitment to have regular meetings on a particular subject.

As a general rule, meetings you're asked to attend due to reasons 1 or 2 are more likely to be useful to you than meetings you're asked to attend due to reasons 3 through 7. However (and unfortunately), you probably will not be able to avoid all the meetings that are not useful to you, especially if they're called by your boss or the coworkers who've got clout.

3. LIMIT YOUR MEETING ATTENDANCE.

As explained above, some meetings are mandatory while others are not. If you're absolutely required to attend a meeting, skip to Step 4.

However, if there's any question as to whether your presence is required, compare your own goals to the meeting's reason and decide whether the benefit of attending is greater than the benefit of doing something else. To make this decision, ask yourself two questions: "What's in it for me?" and "What if I pass on it?"

Example 1:

Your boss's peer has asked the entire division (including his group and your boss's) to attend a meeting where the peer will give the presentation that he's planning to give to top management next week. You ask yourself:

1. *What's in it for me?* I'll get some visibility with my boss's peer and probably my own boss, since she'll probably attend. I may also get a better sense of how the peer approaches problems, which might prove useful in the future. I will also have the opportunity before and after to socialize with coworkers.

2. *What if I pass on it?* Since many of my coworkers might attend, if I don't show up, everyone might wonder why I'm not there. In addition, the boss's peer might take my absence as an insult, making things more difficult for my own boss.

In this case you probably want to attend.

Example 2:

You're an engineering manager whom the marketing group has invited to a group writing session for a press release about a new product design. You ask:

1. *What's in it for me?* I'll be able to prevent the marketing group from saying something stupid or inaccurate.

2. *What if I pass on it?* I won't waste two hours arguing about trivia and they'll have to run the press release by me anyway when they're done.

In this case you pass. Rather than attending, you send an e-mail with the technical specs you think should be included, along with a reminder that you'd like to review the final version before it's released to the press.

After asking the two questions (as shown in the examples above), decide whether it makes sense for you to attend. If it does, skip to Step 4.

If it doesn't make sense for you to attend, create an excuse that's plausible but not insulting.

WRONG:

- "It sounds like a waste of time."
- "I have better things to do."

RIGHT:

- "I have a scheduling conflict."
- "I have to meet a deadline."

4. PREPARE YOURSELF WELL.

If you've gotten to this step, you're definitely attending the meeting. Your goal is now to make certain that you can contribute in a way that reinforces your agenda, even if that only means looking good at the meeting.

Research the background of the topics that will be discussed. This is easy if there's a published agenda. If there isn't, ask whoever called the meeting what will be discussed and how you should best prepare.

For example, suppose you're a marketing manager whose goal is to create advertisements that generate sales leads. You've been asked to a meeting with the sales team to discuss how the company can sell more to the automobile industry.

In accordance with Step 3, you ask yourself:

1. *What's in it for me?* The salespeople may know customers who are willing to endorse us publicly in our advertisements.

2. *What if I pass on it?* It will seem as if marketing doesn't care about the sales team and can't be bothered to help them out.

On the basis of your answers, you decide to attend. Because you're going to be asking the salespeople for a favor (sharing their personal contacts with you), you want to come into the meeting with something that helps the salespeople.

You therefore get online and read up on buying trends in the automobile industry. You now have something substantive to contribute, which will help you work your own agenda (getting the contact names).

5. GATHER YOUR IDEAS.

As the meeting progresses, take notes (either mentally, on your device, or on paper) about what's said. Look for areas of discussion where you might be able to either add value (which will burnish your reputation) or push your own agenda.

These notes are important because when you do say something, you want it to come out as a complete thought, rather than a half-prepared remark that peters out in the middle because you can't remember exactly what you were going to say.

6. READ THE ROOM, THEN CONTRIBUTE.

Novice meeting attendees either blurt out their ideas and opinions at the first break in the conversation or delay saying something until after the meeting has moved on to another topic.

Experienced meeting attendees know that the trick to contributing to a meeting (and looking good in the process) is to make your remarks toward the end of that part of the discussion.

When you express your own view or add your contribution, speak confidently and in complete sentences; then, if appropriate, ask a question that you feel will move the discussion in a direction in which you'd like to see the meeting go.

For example, suppose you're in the marketing/sales meeting described in Step 4. To recap, you want the salespeople to use their contacts to give you reference accounts for an advertisement. In preparation for the meeting, you've researched buying habits in the automotive industry.

During the meeting a salesperson complains that it's difficult to get CEOs of auto-supply firms to return calls. Several other salespeople echo this sentiment. When you sense that the topic is almost exhausted, you say, "My research into buying patterns in the automotive industry says that what really motivates CEOs to buy from a vendor is a recommendation from another CEO. What if we ran an ad featuring a CEO who's our current customer?"

Bringing up your idea at this point—when other people have spoken their minds—is far more likely to result in the support of the other attendees than if, for example, you tried to get your market research, or your request for a reference account, directly onto the agenda.

ATTENDING MEETINGS

- ■ **TREAT** meetings as a possible way to advance your agenda.
- ■ **SOME** types of meetings can be useful; others are usually not.
- ■ **DECIDE** whether each meeting will be useful or useless.
- ■ **EITHER** decline to attend or prepare well; no in-between.
- ■ **TAKE** notes so you can speak coherently when it's your turn.
- ■ **SPEAK** confidently and, if appropriate, segue into your agenda.

PART **III** How to Manage
Your Employees

Although more than a million books have been published on the subject of management, managing employees is not nearly as complicated as the consultants (who write most of the books) try to make it out to be.

Good management is mostly a matter of common sense and a few easily mastered techniques. This part of the book helps make common sense, well, more common. It lays out both the strategic foundation of good management and specific tactics to build and grow a winning team.

Here's what you'll learn:

■ "What Truly Great Bosses Believe" lays out the interlocking and self-reinforcing belief system that is the core of every useful management technique, based on more than thirty years of observing the very best managers in action.

■ "How to Be a Better Boss" gives twelve essential rules to ensure that you continue to focus on what's really important—managing people—even when other concerns vie to capture your attention.

- "How to Hire a Top Performer" addresses the all-important task of finding the best people to be on your team. When you've got the right people, good management becomes far easier.

- "How to Hold a Productive Meeting" provides guidelines for keeping your meetings on track and moving toward a goal, without consuming time and effort that could better be spent elsewhere.

- "How to Offer Criticism" explains how to start a conversation about problematic behavior in a way that doesn't offend the employee but instead lays the groundwork for a change in that employee's behavior.

- "How to Redirect a Complainer" shows how to help employees who are stuck on a problem move gradually into finding their own solution, taking your advice, or focusing on something more productive.

- "How to Fire Somebody" covers the most difficult task you'll ever undertake at work: telling an employee that he or she no longer has a job, with a minimum of damage to the employee, yourself, and the rest of the team.

15

What Truly Great Bosses Believe

The most successful bosses—and the ones employees respect and follow most easily, and who are most likely to be promoted—tend to share the following eight core beliefs:

1. BUSINESS IS AN ECOSYSTEM, NOT A BATTLEFIELD.

Average bosses see business as a conflict among companies, departments, and groups. They build armies of troops to order about, demonize competitors as "enemies," and treat customers as territory to be conquered.

Great bosses see business as a symbiosis through which the most diverse firm is most likely to survive and thrive. They create teams that adapt easily to new markets and can quickly form partnerships with other companies, customers...and even competitors.

2. A COMPANY IS A COMMUNITY, NOT A MACHINE.

Average bosses consider their companies machines with employees as cogs. They create rigid structures with rigid rules and then try to maintain control by pulling levers and steering the ship.

Great bosses see their companies as collections of individual hopes and dreams, all connected to a higher purpose. They inspire employees to dedicate themselves to the success of their peers and therefore to the community—and company—at large.

3. MANAGEMENT IS SERVICE, NOT CONTROL.

Average bosses want employees to do exactly what they're told. They're hyper-aware of anything that smacks of insubordination and create environments in which individual initiative is squelched by the "wait and see what the boss says" mentality.

Great bosses set a general direction and then commit to obtaining the resources their employees need to get the job done. They push decision-making downward, allowing teams to form their own rules, and intervene only in emergencies.

4. EMPLOYEES ARE PEERS, NOT CHILDREN.

Average bosses see employees as inferior, immature beings who simply can't be trusted if not overseen by a patriarchal management. Employees take their cues from this attitude and expend energy on looking busy and covering their behinds.

Great bosses treat every employee as if he or she were the most important person in the firm. Excellence is expected everywhere, from the loading dock to the boardroom, and as a result, employees do their best work for themselves, the boss, and the company.

5. MOTIVATION COMES FROM VISION, NOT FEAR.

Average bosses see fear—of getting fired, of ridicule, of loss of privilege—as a crucial means of motivating people. As a result, employees and managers alike become paralyzed and unable to make risky decisions, even when those decisions are crucial to the survival of the firm.

Great bosses inspire people to see a better future and how they'll be a part of it. Employees work harder when they believe in the organization's goals, truly enjoy what they're doing, and (of course) know they'll share in the rewards.

6. CHANGE EQUALS GROWTH, NOT PAIN.

Average bosses see change as both complicated and threatening, something to be endured only when a firm is in desperate shape. They subconsciously torpedo change...until it's too late.

Great bosses see change as an inevitable part of life. While they don't value change for its own sake, they know that success is possible only if employees and organizations embrace new ideas and new ways of doing business.

7. TECHNOLOGY OFFERS EMPOWERMENT, NOT AUTOMATION.

Average bosses adhere to the old IT-centric view that technology is primarily a means of strengthening management control and increasing predictability. They install centralized computer systems that remove decision-making power from the employees.

Great bosses see technology as a means of freeing people to be more creative and to build better and stronger relationships. When working with the IT group, they adapt back-office systems to the tools, such as smartphones and tablets, that people actually want to use.

8. WORK SHOULD BE FUN, NOT MERE TOIL.

Average bosses buy into the notion that work is, at best, a necessary evil. They fully expect employees to resent having to work, and therefore tend to subconsciously define themselves as oppressors and their employees as victims. Everyone then behaves accordingly.

Great bosses see work as something that should be inherently enjoyable, and therefore believe one of the most important jobs of a manager is to, as far as possible, put people in jobs that make them happy, so more work gets done.

SHORTCUT

BELIEVING AS GREAT MANAGERS DO

■ BUSINESS is an ecosystem so cooperate, don't fight.

■ COMPANIES are communities so treat people as individuals.

■ MANAGEMENT is service so make others successful first.

■ EMPLOYEES are your peers so treat them like adults.

■ MOTIVATE with vision because fear only paralyzes.

■ CHANGE is growth so welcome rather than shun it.

■ TECHNOLOGY eliminates busywork and frees creativity.

■ WORK is fun so don't turn it into a chore.

16

How to Be a Better Boss

Over the years I've worked with dozens of managers and interviewed hundreds more. As I consider how they approach their jobs and how they characterize their successes, I've noticed they tend to adhere to the following rules:

1. MANAGE INDIVIDUALS, NOT NUMBERS.

Conventional business thinking is that what's important is slicing and dicing the numbers, putting the numbers into graphs, and talking about where the numbers are and where they ought to be.

However, numbers are the result of how well you manage people, not how well you manage numbers. The only way to get better numbers (regardless of your measurements scheme) is to improve the performance of the individuals who work for you.

2. ADAPT YOUR STYLE TO THE INDIVIDUAL.

Despite the popularity of the phrase, in fact it's impossible to "manage people." You can only manage individuals. Since everyone is unique, there is no one-size-fits-all management style.

Therefore, as you explain exactly what you want from each employee, actively solicit the employee's suggestions and ideas about how you can get the best possible work from that person.

3. ADOPT SIMPLE AND RELEVANT METRICS.

While your main focus needs to be individuals rather than numbers, you still need a way to measure how well those individuals are doing. Complex measurement schemes, with multiple metrics, inevitably create confusion among employees and managers alike.

Ideally what's being measured should be simple enough for every employee to understand at a glance, and relate as closely as possible to the behaviors that you're trying to encourage. If the work doesn't affect the metrics, metrics are a waste of time.

4. SET ONE PRIORITY PER INDIVIDUAL.

I recently received an e-mail from someone whose boss assigned multiple tasks and insisted that each was a "huge priority." That boss was an idiot, because if *everything* is a priority, then *nothing* is a priority.

The entire concept of a priority is that *one* thing is more important than everything else. Giving your employees multiple priorities is foisting on them the responsibility of deciding what's really important. That's *your* job.

5. KEEP YOUR TEMPER.

When you explode at an employee, or make a cutting or hurtful remark, it creates a wound that never heals completely and that festers with secret resentment. You don't have to be perfect, but your employees are *not* your punching bags.

Employees despise bosses who are so emotionally weak they have to dump their anger and frustration onto others. By contrast, employees deeply appreciate a boss who remains calm in a crisis.

6. MEASURE YOURSELF BY YOUR WEAKEST EMPLOYEE.

Managers use their top performers as a measure of how successful they are as leaders. However, while you may have a top performer on your team, that success is more likely to reflect his or her drive and ability rather than anything you brought to the table.

Measure your management ability based on how you handle your worst performers. It's those employees who define the lowest level of performance you're willing to tolerate, and how much you expect the other employees to compensate for your low standards.

7. BE GENEROUS.

Being generous is not just about money; it's about how you treat people. Smart bosses know their real job is to (1) fix the failures before they happen, (2) publicize the wins employees achieve, and (3) take the heat when things go wrong.

Money is what employees expect from their *jobs*, not their bosses. Employees want bosses to be generous with information, time, praise, and the coaching that teaches employees how to do their jobs better.

8. DON'T BE A KNOW-IT-ALL.

Many bosses wrongly believe their job is to be the expert and know all the answers. However, when managers provide all the answers, they rob their employees of the opportunity to *think* and *grow*.

While experience has value, people can't learn when wisdom is presented on a platter or forced down their throats. Employees respect bosses who admit they don't know everything and ask questions that help spark an employee's own creativity.

9. DON'T PLAY FAVORITES.

Since you're human, you're going to like some of your employees better than others. Even so, you must not let these personal preferences become an excuse for treating those you like differently from those you don't.

Playing a favorite demoralizes the other employees because they know that their best work won't count as much. In addition, playing a favorite creates a lot of hostility toward the favorite. If you remember from school, the teacher's pet usually got clobbered on the playground.

10. GIVE LOYALTY TO GET LOYALTY.

As a boss, you want your employees to watch out for your interests, help you to be successful, and not leave you in the lurch the second they find a better job. In other words, you want some loyalty.

Loyalty, however, must be earned. You can only expect employees to be loyal to you if you're willing to first be loyal to them. That means watching out for their interests, helping them to be successful, and keeping them on board even if you can hire someone else for less.

11. BE REASONABLY TRANSPARENT.

Some bosses play their cards close to the chest and never let employees in on the decision-making process. By contrast, smart bosses know that decisions are more successful when those tasked with their implementation are involved from the start.

A boss who disappears into his or her office, makes a decision, and then emerges with a set of commands leaves the impression that the decision is arbitrary. Even if they don't like a decision, employees far prefer to understand the workings of the boss's mind and exactly why that decision was made.

12. MAKE DECISIONS QUICKLY.

Some bosses are so risk-averse that they require mountains of information before making any important decision. Smart bosses, on the other hand, understand there's a point (and it usually comes fairly quickly) at which additional information merely muddies the waters.

Obsessing about (and second-guessing) your decision-making is always a waste of time. You're better off making a good enough decision than waiting for an imaginary perfect decision to emerge from a real-world situation.

BEING A BETTER BOSS

- **MANAGE** individuals, not numbers.
- **ADAPT** your style to each person.
- **MEASURE** what's truly relevant.
- **ONLY** one priority per person.
- **STAY** even-tempered.
- **TAKE** responsibility for your low performers.
- **SHARE** your thoughts and ideas.
- **ASK** questions rather than providing answers.
- **TREAT** everyone as equally as possible.
- **DON'T** expect more than you're willing to give.
- **EXPLAIN** the reasoning behind your decisions.
- **DON'T** prevaricate, decide now!

17

How to Hire a Top Performer

You can't be a great boss if you don't hire the right people. You don't just want people who can do the job—you want people who will excel and whose contributions will help you and your firm be more successful. Here's how:

1. HAVE A PARAGON IN MIND.

Study your best employees to determine the characteristics that differentiate them from the average ones. Find out what drives your best people to be the best. Discover which talents and skills are crucial to success in your unique business environment.

Then create interview questions that will reveal whether the candidate can be exceptional in your specific organization.

2. ALWAYS BE INTERVIEWING.

It's absurd to expect somebody extraordinary to walk through the door when you want them to. Rather than wait until your moment of greatest need, interview candidates all the time, even if you don't have any job openings.

Use a combination of e-mail and social networking to keep in touch with the best applicants. That way you'll have exceptional candidates ready when you have a spot for them.

3. ASK QUESTIONS THAT REVEAL CHARACTER.

You can't identify somebody extraordinary by asking ordinary interview questions. Rather than something like "What is your greatest achievement?" ask the candidate to write down some achievements—two from grade school, two from high school, two from college, and two post-college—with at least one being business-related.

Then ask which achievement makes the candidate proudest. This will let you delve into his or her core motivations.

4. SEEK PEOPLE WHO HAVE OVERCOME DISAPPOINTMENT.

Extraordinary employees are resilient—a character trait that emerges only from life experience. When you're interviewing, probe for defining moments when the candidate encountered disappointments and yet managed to move forward.

Exceptional employees will have personal experiences that illustrate their resilience, which helps employees shrug off the frustrations that are part of any high-performance job.

5. DON'T CONFUSE SUCCESS WITH MOTIVATION.

Many people are successful only when somebody else is providing the motivation. For example, many top athletes (even Olympians!) slack off when a coach is not "riding herd." This is not necessarily a bad thing, but maintaining that level of coaching will take a lot of effort on your part.

So unless you plan to spend a lot of your time providing motivation, look for employees who haven't depended on the constant attention of a boss to be successful.

6. HIRE FOR ATTITUDE RATHER THAN EXPERIENCE.

Experience can be misleading, especially in a business environment, where things are always changing. As many hiring managers have learned (to their dismay), some "experienced" candidates have just had the same bad experience over and over.

Rather than focusing on what candidates did in the past, focus on whether they have the attitude and basic skills that will make them extraordinary in the future.

7. GET A REAL RECOMMENDATION.

Extraordinary employees are usually likable—but plenty of likable people are particularly good at convincing employers that they have talents they don't actually possess.

Never hire a candidate unless you've talked to somebody who says you'd be crazy *not* to hire that person. Ideally you should research and locate the reference yourself, rather than simply calling the ones on the candidate's résumé.

SHORTCUT

HIRING TOP PERFORMERS

- ■ **KNOW** exactly whom you're looking for.
- ■ **CONSTANTLY** seek viable candidates.
- ■ **LOOK** for character, not experience.
- ■ **RESILIENCE** is the mark of potential greatness.
- ■ **SEEK** out the self-motivated.
- ■ **ATTITUDE** is all-important.
- ■ **DON'T** settle for canned references.

How to Hold a Productive Meeting

If you're the boss, it's very much in your interest to have short meetings that work toward a goal as quickly as possible, so your employees can get back to doing real work. Here's how to keep your meetings brief and to the point:

1. HAVE AN AGENDA.

Many useless meetings have amorphous goals such as "sharing information." However, unless you've got time to waste, it's crazy to tie people up in a meeting unless there's something important to be decided on.

If you can't pinpoint why you're calling a meeting, don't call it. Once you do know why you're calling the meeting, create an agenda that explains the goal of the meeting and the steps that are to be taken at the meeting to achieve that goal. For example:

Meeting goal: Decide how to proceed on the Acme account.

1. Discuss current status.
2. Brainstorm how to get back on target.
3. Reach agreement on recommendations.

2. PROVIDE BACKGROUND INFORMATION.

If you want your meetings to go quickly, avoid disseminating information via PowerPoint presentations. In most cases it's more efficient for people to skim that information than to have it spoon-fed from the podium.

To avoid unnecessary presentations, create briefing documents that can be scanned quickly either before or during the meeting, and that provide sufficient information that attendees can intelligently discuss the issues on the agenda.

It may not be practical to completely avoid presentations, but presumably everybody at the meeting knows how to read. Think of it this way: if a meeting is important enough to hold, it's important enough to have a background document for attendees to read beforehand.

3. STAY ON TARGET.

If you've followed the first three steps, there's no reason *any* meeting should last more than an hour. An hour is about as long as most people can focus on a single subject anyway, which is why most college classes are an hour long.

If the meeting starts to meander, yank it back to the agenda. Table any new issues that surface for another meeting. If latecomers barge in, don't waste everyone else's time catching them up.

By the way, some people come late to meetings specifically to show that they're important by making everyone else wait. Refusing to go over material that's already been discussed squelches this annoying behavior before it gets out of hand.

4. DISTRIBUTE THE MINUTES.

If the meeting was important enough to hold, it was important enough to document the results of the meeting. Meeting minutes should therefore be distributed to the attendees while the meeting is still fresh in their minds.

The minutes should begin with a statement of whether the meeting achieved its goal. The minutes should match the agenda, thereby documenting whether the meeting goal was achieved. Example:

Meeting goal: Decide how to proceed on the Acme account.

1. Acme has a temporary freeze on new purchases, which is delaying the sale of our widget inventory.

2. Two main approaches to breaking the logjam were discussed. The first approach is a one-time-only discount that might convince Acme to buy now. The second approach is to meet with Acme's CFO to discuss making an exception.

3. The consensus at the meeting was that a discount would create a bad precedent. Instead we will have our CFO call Acme's CFO to discuss the situation and propose a meeting.

4. We will provide the results of that call via e-mail prior to our next meeting.

SHORTCUT

MAKING MEETINGS PRODUCTIVE

- **HAVE** an agenda before you meet.
- **PROVIDE** background information.
- **DON'T** let the meeting meander.
- **DOCUMENT** what decisions were made.

How to Offer Criticism

Praising good performance is easy because everyone likes to receive compliments. But what do you do when a kick in the butt is more appropriate than a pat on the back? Here's how to do this effectively:

1. ADDRESS PROBLEMATIC BEHAVIORS QUICKLY.

Criticism is best given in real time or immediately after the fact. If you wait until problems fester, you only end up making those problems worse, because the other person becomes accustomed to the problematic behavior.

For example, suppose an employee shows up in an outfit that's inappropriate for your workplace. If you let the matter slide, there's a good chance the employee will dress similarly in the future and be all the more embarrassed when you finally object.

2. IDENTIFY THE BEHAVIOR YOU WANT CHANGED.

Because your goal is to change a behavior, it's counterproductive to bring up and discuss the personality issues that you might believe lie behind the behavior. When you attempt to address personality issues, you're making a direct assault on the other person's self-image, thereby guaranteeing a defensive reaction. Example:

- *You*: You're unreliable! You've been late three times this week!
- *Employee*: I'm not unreliable! That's not fair!

Criticism of behavior is easier for people to accept and act on when it's accompanied by some praise. You do not do this to sugarcoat the criticism but to recognize that the other person had good intentions, regardless of the behavior.

So start with some praise and then segue to the behavior you want changed using the conjunction *and* rather than the more commonly used conjunction *but*.

WRONG:

- "You're a big contributor to our success *but* you're exploding in anger when people question your ideas."

RIGHT:

- "You're a big contributor to our success *and* you're exploding in anger when people question your ideas."

Note that the use of *but* turns the praise into a backhanded insult while the use of *and* tends to reinforce the compliment.

3. USE QUESTIONS TO MOVE THE DIALOGUE FORWARD.

Now that you've surfaced the behavior you want changed, you want to get the employee involved in, and committed to, changing that behavior. That's possible only if you know the deeper roots of the behavior you want changed.

When you listen to somebody and acknowledge what he or she has to say, you learn about the world from that person's point of view, which helps you better analyze how to help an employee change his or her behavior. Example:

- *You*: You're usually a great employee and you've been late three times this week. What's up?
- *Employee*: I'm having problems with my child-care provider.
- *You*: You're obviously committed to being a good parent, and I need you here on time or everyone else's work falls behind. How can we address this problem?

4. GET COMMITMENT ON AN ACTION PLAN.

Resolve any differences between your perception of the situation and the employee's perception of the situation. Gain agreement on the area where there is a gap between the employee's performance and what's required.

Ideally the employee will come up with a plan to address the behavior. If not, or if the solution seems insufficient, provide your perspective on how to address the problem. Decide together what needs to be done in order to change the behavior. Example:

- *You*: You did a great job on that test program and I'm hearing that you've been expressing some anger in your e-mails to the programming staff. What's up?
- *Employee*: It really pisses me off when the programmers blame the errors on the test program rather than their own inability to write good code.
- *You*: I can tell you're passionate about eliminating the errors and I think you'd get better cooperation if you dialed down the anger a bit. Any ideas?
- *Employee*: Well, I suppose I could drink less coffee...
- *You*: Good idea. Maybe you could commit to waiting a day before sending any e-mail that you write when you're angry. Can you do that?
- *Employee*: Yeah, I guess so.
- *You*: Great.

5. FOLLOW UP CONSISTENTLY.

It takes time for people to change their behavior because old habits die hard. Unless the other person is very motivated to do something different, it's likely that he or she will slip back into the problematic behavior.

Continue to reinforce the new behaviors by monitoring performance and providing additional coaching as necessary. Don't give up until the person you're coaching has achieved his or her potential.

SHORTCUT

CRITICIZING EMPLOYEES

- **ADDRESS** undesirable behaviors when they happen.
- **OFFER** praise, then identify the behavior you want changed.
- **ASK** questions to understand the "why" behind the behavior.
- **AGREE** upon a plan to change the behavior.
- **MONITOR** and reinforce the changed behavior.

How to Redirect a Complainer

In an ideal world, employees would spend more time solving problems than grousing about them. But the real world, unfortunately, contains many people who would rather complain than take action.

Complainers make it more difficult for everyone to get their jobs done. They not only waste their own time in complaining, but they eat up your time whenever you get stuck listening to their grievances. Here's how to handle them:

1. SCHEDULE A CONVERSATION.

If a known complainer (and you know who they are) comes into your work area and indicates that he or she wants to talk, do *not* interrupt what you're doing in order to have the conversation.

Instead, explain that you do want to hear what the person has to say, but that you can't give the matter the attention it deserves while your mind is on your current task. Schedule a specific time in the not-too-distant future.

There are several advantages to this:

1. It limits the impact of the complainer on your productivity.

2. It prevents the complainer from using your sympathetic ear as a way to avoid doing his or her own work.

3. It conveys respect for the complainer and a willingness to listen... at the appropriate time.

When the scheduled time rolls around, there'll be a chance the complainer has been distracted by something else, in which case, *problem solved*. But if not, go to Step 2.

2. SET THE AGENDA.

Start the scheduled conversation with this question: "As we discuss this, do you want me to suggest solutions or do you just need to vent for a while?" This question is essential for three reasons:

1. It recognizes the fact that some people can't begin to think about a solution until they've complained about the problem for a while.

2. It establishes that there is probably a solution to whatever the complainer is complaining about, even if this isn't the right time to surface it.

3. It sets a time limit for the complaining, thereby making certain that it doesn't become a productivity hole.

3. LISTEN TO THE COMPLAINT.

Regardless of whether the complainer claims to want a solution, once he or she begins complaining, resist the urge to provide a solution (at least for now). Remember, *complainers above all need to feel that they're being heard.*

Even if the complaints seem ridiculous and pointless, do not roll your eyes, fidget, or check your e-mail. Instead, nod your head and say things like "I hear you," or "That must be really tough."

In most cases the complainer will peter out in five minutes or less, as long as you don't add fuel to the fire by prematurely suggesting a solution. When the complainer falls silent, ask questions that address how he or she feels:

- "When you think about this, what else comes to mind?"
- "What drove you to bring this to my attention now?"
- "Are you ready to consider a workable solution?"

These questions help the complainer start visualizing a way to solve the problem, rather than merely complain about it.

4. ASK WHAT THE COMPLAINER PLANS TO DO.

Getting the entire problem onto the table usually helps the complainer see what he or she needs to do to address it, even if it's just something as simple as sucking it up and moving on.

Most complainers already know what they need to do to address the problem—but can't motivate themselves to take action until they've moaned about it for a while. So sometimes complainers will say, "I don't know what to do."

If this happens, respond with, "Well, if you did know what to do, what would that be?" This restatement of the question can often short-circuit self-induced helplessness.

If the complainer has an idea, listen quietly as before. If the complainer remains stuck on "I don't know what do to," say something like, "I can tell you're really frustrated." Then move to the next step.

5. CONFIRM THAT YOUR ADVICE IS TRULY WANTED.

Once the complainer has vented and wound down, ask, "Did it help to get that off your chest?" Whether the answer is yes, no, or maybe is irrelevant. This question is intended only to establish that you've listened to the complaint.

Because you listened to the complaint, the complainer now *owes* you. That's both good and appropriate, because listening to complainers is hard work. Now ask the all-important question: "Do you want my perspective on the situation?"

If the answer is no, let the matter drop, feeling secure that, by listening, you've done what you could to help the complainer get back on track. If the answer is yes, move to the next step.

6. PROVIDE YOUR BEST ADVICE.

Start by saying something like this: "I'm going to give you my opinion on how you should address this problem. After I do, I'm willing to answer questions about how you might implement it, but that's all."

Provide your best advice, incorporating (when practical) whatever suggestions the employee surfaced in Step 4. Phrase the advice from your own point of view. Say something like, "If I were in your situation, I might..."

Then ask, "Any questions?" If the complainer starts explaining why your advice won't work (aka "Yeah, but..."), hold up your hands, palm outward, and say, "That's my best advice." End the meeting.

If the complainer responds with implementation questions, answer them to the best of your ability. And congratulations, because you've turned a complainer into a problem-solver.

Note that by following these steps you've shown not only respect for the complainer (or ex-complainer, as the case may be), but also that you're not willing to participate in a whining session.

How to Fire Somebody

The hardest job for any manager is firing somebody (even if that person isn't right for the job) or, worse, laying off multiple employees when they've done nothing to deserve it. There's no way to make this process easy, but here's how to make it less traumatic:

1. DON'T USE WEASEL WORDS.

Words such as *downsizing* and *rightsizing* are intended to make managers feel better because they tend to mask the fact that real human beings are involved. It's like when military organizations say *collateral damage* when they mean *dead civilians*.

Even phrases such as *letting people go* exhibit management gutlessness. It's as if the managers are pretending that the "people" were champing at the bit to leave and management is finally giving them what they want.

If you're firing somebody, say, "I'm firing you." If you're having layoffs, call them layoffs. Tell it like it is, even if the truth is hard to say. After all, the truth is going to be even harder on the people who are losing their jobs.

2. YOU MIGHT BE NEXT.

Because firing people is such an unpleasant job, it's not at all unusual for a big boss to ask a lower-level manager to do the dirty work, and then fire that manager. From the big boss's perspective, this turns a series of hard tasks into one relatively easy one.

Treat your soon-to-be-ex-employees as decently as possible, if only because you may run into them in the unemployment line.

3. GIVE HONEST REASONS, IF POSSIBLE.

You owe your employees a real reason they're losing their jobs. Don't dance around the truth. By the way, most of the time, the real reason for a layoff is "Your management, including me, screwed up."

That being said, you may not have the option of acting like a decent human being, because of legal restrictions and government regulations. To keep yourself from being caught in the middle and possibly making things worse for yourself and everyone else, follow whatever corporate policy has been made in terms of what you can say to the people you're firing.

4. BE QUICK AND THOROUGH.

Firings and layoffs should be handled like a life-threatening operation at a hospital. You want the patient (i.e., your firm) to get through trauma as quickly as possible, not bleed the death of a thousand cuts.

Do the firings or the layoffs quickly, so everybody can move past them. This is very much in your interest because if the process is drawn out, your best people (the ones you would never want to fire) may get nervous and find employment elsewhere.

In any case, your remaining employees (especially the top performers) will feel weird and uncomfortable because they're still employed while their erstwhile colleagues have departed. Make certain the survivors know they're valued, and help them make the transition.

WHEN FIRING OR LAYING OFF

- ▓ **TELL** it like it is without the biz-blab.
- ▓ **SHOW** empathy for your coworkers.
- ▓ **EXPLAIN** why it's happening, as far as you can.
- ▓ **CUT** quickly, heal, and move on.

IV

How to Manage Yourself

Of all the relationships you'll have at work, the most important is your relationship with yourself. Your success in the workplace depends directly on how well you manage the only two things over which you have any real control: your mind and your body.

Companies now demand that employees to do more in less time, and those who survive are often tasked with carrying the workload of those who have been laid off. As never before, it's up to you to make your own future.

This part of the book provides the secrets you'll need to consistently and easily advance your career:

■ "How to Achieve Career Security" explains how to make yourself more valuable to your current employer and better able to find another job, thereby making yourself more effective in dealing with bosses and coworkers alike.

■ "How to Have Enough Time" contains the surprising secret to managing time, thereby creating less stress at work, and providing yourself with the breathing room you need to pursue your highest goals.

■ "How to Find Your Dream Job" provides a system for finding the kind of job and career that will suit you best. You'll learn why most people never achieve a dream job and what you'll need to do to be the exception to the rule.

■ "How to Land a Job Interview" explains how to get the inside track and separate yourself from the crowd of job seekers. You'll also learn exactly why sending out hundreds of résumés never works.

■ "How to Ace a Job Interview" shows how to prepare yourself and conduct yourself so job interviewers see you as an ideal candidate. It also explains why the questions you ask can be more important than the ones you answer.

■ "How to Make Failure Impossible" provides a step-by-step process for using every bit of your work experience to lead you toward your goals. While no method can guarantee success, this process does guarantee that you'll never be a loser.

■ "How to Become More Optimistic" gives easy tips and techniques to create an attitude that will keep you motivated and positive, both when things are going your way and when you'd prefer they go differently.

22

How to Achieve Career Security

In a world of globalization and outsourcing, nobody can achieve *job* security. However, it is possible to put yourself in a position where (1) your employer will be reluctant to fire you and (2) you can easily find another job. I call this *career security*, and here's how to achieve it:

1. GET INTO A DEFENSIVE FINANCIAL POSITION.

If you're barely keeping the proverbial wolf from the door, you'll feel trapped in your current job, because losing it would create instant hardship.

Because of this, career security means being in a financial position where you can be totally unemployed for at least six months without having to greatly change your living arrangements.

I fully realize that this is difficult for some people to achieve, especially if they're already loaded down with student loan debt, mortgages, and so forth. Even so, it's essential because you want to accept the best possible job (rather than the first job that comes along), and you don't want to be distracted by moving, bankruptcy, etc. while job hunting.

It may take some time to get yourself into this position, but it's definitely worth it, even if it means living with a roommate or at your parents', never eating out, shopping at thrift stores, etc.

2. MAKE YOURSELF LESS REPLACEABLE.

No company employs people at a financial loss. Chances are that you're producing far more value for your company than it's spending on your compensation (salary, bonuses, commissions, perks, etc.).

In a financial sense, you can best calculate your value to your firm by looking at how expensive it would be replace you. (I discuss how to do this in "Secret 5. How to Ask for a Raise.") It's very much in your interest to increase your replacement cost.

You accomplish this by achieving unusual expertise in some area of the company's operations. The more you can contribute regularly to the success of the company, the less likely you are to be replaced.

Companies value three types of expertise:

1. *Deep expertise.* This entails mastering one or more complex and specialized skills. For example, if you're a computer programmer, you might want to become an expert in an obscure but essential programming language.

2. *Broad expertise.* This entails developing business acumen that allows you to play a wide variety of roles. Bosses are reluctant to let go of "utility players" because they'd have to hire multiple people to do the same work.

3. *Network expertise.* This entails building such a strong network of relationships that your departure would damage the firm financially. For instance, a top salesperson might take some customer accounts with her when she leaves.

Suppose you're a new hire in a marketing group that's doing corporate branding. To make yourself less replaceable you might have three choices:

1. *Deep expertise.* Learn everything you can about developing brand awareness through the use of multiple social media platforms.

2. *Broad expertise.* Develop skills (and take on projects) that span the entire realm of brand marketing.

3. *Network expertise.* Build relationships with your engineers and customers so both groups look to you as their ally.

Similarly, suppose you're a manufacturing engineer with twenty-five years of experience. To make yourself less replaceable you might have three choices:

1. *Deep expertise.* Become the only person in the company who understands the software that runs the factory floor.

2. *Broad expertise.* Become the overall manager of the technical aspects of the manufacturing system.

3. *Network expertise.* Become the technical contact for the companies in your supply chain.

3. CREATE A WRITTEN ESCAPE PLAN.

In addition to making yourself less replaceable, spend at least two hours every week (schedule them!) finding new business contacts, developing those relationships, and keeping abreast of opportunities in your field.

Your goal is to constantly have multiple job opportunities in various stages of development. Having such alternatives lined up provides four advantages:

1. You will have the courage to say no to unreasonable requests.
2. You will be more willing to risk your job in order to do the right thing.
3. You will eventually find a job that's better than the one you've got.

4. You will be unafraid to ask for compensation that reflects your true value.

As you develop these contacts and opportunities, put them in the form of an escape plan, detailing what you'd do and whom you'd call if you suddenly lost your job. There are three advantages to having a written escape plan:

1. It helps you visualize the process, which will make it easier if you ever need to execute the plan.

2. It makes it unnecessary for you to worry about what you'd do in the event that you lose your job.

3. It provides a vehicle for documenting the contacts you make and the opportunities you're developing.

Example:

Potential employer: Microfirm

How I could add value: I use their products in my current job, so I could help them develop new customer opportunities.

Contacts:
- John Doe, marketing manager, 210-555-1543, jd@microfirm.net.
- Jane Eyre, system architect, 210-555-1553, je@microfirm.net.

Actions:
- Met John at the EDA conference in June 2012, discussed new products.
- Commented on Jane's blog on subject of new instruction set.

- Briefly discussed their future needs on phone call with John, 7/5/13.

Ideally you want to be developing *at least three* of these opportunities at every point in your career. In other words, while you've got job A, you should simultaneously be developing job opportunities B, C, and D.

SHORTCUT

CAREER SECURITY

- **LIVE** below your means until you've saved six months of income.

- **DEVELOP** expertise that makes it less likely you'll be fired.

- **CONSTANTLY** develop new opportunities and document them in a written escape plan.

23

How to Have Enough Time

Even though most people complain that they haven't enough time, it's actually easy to have enough time to get all your work done, and still have time left over for a personal life. The secret is as follows:

1. STOP COMPLAINING.

You get the same amount of time every day as everyone else. You may feel you're short on time and that you desperately need more, but when the day started, you got your fair share: twenty-four hours.

Nobody got any more than you did, so stop complaining. More important, the time you're wasting by complaining could be spent doing something productive.

2. TRACK YOUR TIME.

Contrary to popular belief, the most difficult part of time management isn't changing the things you do...it's having the courage and discipline to track what you're actually doing. It's a perfect case of "knowledge is power."

Here's the thing: once you realize where you're spending your time, it becomes absurdly easy to determine where you're wasting it.

Simple awareness helps you decide what's a priority and what can be eliminated or delegated to somebody else.

3. LEARN THE PARETO PRINCIPLE.

The Pareto principle is a mathematical law that applies in most situations. The law is as follows: 80 percent of your results come from 20 percent of your actions. Commit this rule to memory, because it's the key to time management.

The most famous example of the Pareto principle is the oft-repeated fact that in sales groups, 80 percent of the revenue comes from 20 percent of the team. There are dozens of other examples, ranging from wealth distribution to damage from natural disasters.

The flip side of this principle is that 80 percent of your actions are producing only 20 percent of your results. Translation: most (i.e., 80 percent) of what you're actually doing is pretty much a waste of time.

4. PRIORITIZE YOUR TO-DO LIST.

The reason most time-management systems don't work is that they tend to treat the 20 percent of your actions that really matter as equivalent to the 80 percent of your actions that aren't actually all that important.

Instead, whenever you make a to-do list, prioritize each item by the amount of effort required, numbering them from 1 to 10, with 1 being the least amount of effort and 10 the most. Then estimate the potential positive results, again from 1 to 10.

Divide the effort by the potential. The result is the "priority ranking." Now do the items with the *lowest* priority number first. For example:

Task 1: Write report on trip meeting
Effort=10, Result=2, Priority=5 (that is, 10÷2)

Task 2: Prepare presentation for marketing
Effort=4, Result=4, Priority=1
Task 3: Call current customer about referral
Effort=1, Result=10, Priority=0.1

5. DO ONLY THE 20 PERCENT THAT REALLY MATTERS.

In order to take advantage of the Pareto principle, you'd do the above tasks in the following order:

- Task 3: Call current customer about referral (Priority 0.1)
- Task 2: Prepare presentation for marketing (Priority 1)
- Task 1: Write report on trip meeting (Priority 5)

Guess what? If you never get to the priority 5 item, it's no big deal. It's probably part of the 80 percent that doesn't really matter.

I know this all sounds pretty simple, even simplistic. However, I can tell you from my personal experience that there has been nothing—and I mean nothing—that has added to my personal productivity more than this kind of prioritization.

Hint: laying out your activities over the next two weeks helps you to finalize and reorganize the plan for the current week. That way you can decide what to pull into this week and what you can push out until next week, or even later.

6. AVOID THESE HUGE TIME-WASTERS.

An easy way to do only what's important is to cut out activities that consume large amounts of time but very seldom pay off big. Here are the four most common:

1. *Taking calls from people you don't know.* Unless you're working in telesales or product support, there's no reason you should ever take a call from somebody you don't know. After all, when was the last

time you took an unexpected call that was truly important? Days? Weeks? Months? If it's important, they'll get you through e-mail.

2. *Accessing voice mail.* A voice mail message consumes minutes of your time (more if you have to replay) to communicate information you could absorb from an e-mail in seconds. Explain in your outgoing message that you don't use voice mail and provide your e-mail address. This alone can save you several hours a month.

3. *Chitchatting with coworkers.* For some people a day at work means an endless coffee break. They wander the halls searching for somebody, ostensibly to discuss business but really just to chat. Don't let these time leeches hobble your success. Just say no. If necessary, get rude if it gets them out of your office.

4. *Letting "alerts" interrupt your thinking.* Most of the 20 percent that makes a real difference involves doing something creative, talking to somebody important, or absorbing complex information. These are impossible to do well if your computer and phone are chirping and beeping for your attention. Whatever it is, it can wait.

SHORTCUT

TIME MANAGEMENT

- ■ **YOU** get twenty-four hours each day, just like everyone else.
- ■ **KEEPING** track of how you spend time is half the battle.
- ■ **TWENTY** percent of your actions will produce 80 percent of your results.
- ■ **PRIORITIZE** based on potential impact and ease of execution.
- ■ **DO** only the 20 percent that produces the 80 percent of your results.
- ■ **AVOID** workplace bustle that consumes time needlessly.

24

How to Find Your Dream Job

Most people blunder their way into their careers—they see an opportunity open up, maybe they've got nothing better going on, maybe they need some money, or maybe they figure this job is good enough for now.

Rather than let yourself accept that fate, you should create a plan to get the perfect job. However—and I want to be very clear on this—you don't have to land your dream job in order to use the other secrets in this book.

Quite the contrary. If you *do* land a dream job, some of the secrets (like those about coping with difficult bosses and coworkers) are likely to be, if not totally unnecessary, at least less important than to somebody struggling with a less-than-ideal job.

There are six steps to finding a dream job:

1. HAVE A DREAM JOB IN MIND.

At various parties, conferences, and get-togethers, I've asked hundreds of people, "If you could have any job you wanted, what would it be?" Almost every time the answer is something like: "Uhhh...I don't know..."

It should seem pretty obvious that if you don't have a clear idea of what constitutes your dream job, the likelihood of getting it is exactly nil, because even if by some insane chance you get offered that dream job, you won't recognize it.

The first step toward getting a dream job is knowing what that job would be. Here's a hint: in most cases your dream job will be connected with whatever truly interests you and makes you happy.

2. START THINKING LIKE YOUR ROLE MODELS.

Just about every "how to succeed" book suggests that you find a role model. Unfortunately, many people use role models in a way that guarantees failure: they imitate the *strategies* that the role models used to get to where they are.

The problem with this approach is that what worked twenty years ago won't work today.

For example, if you wanted to be a film director, you might try to break into the film business the way Steven Spielberg did it: by hanging around a film studio as an unpaid intern.

There's only one problem with this...no, two. First, everybody else is trying to do the same thing, because they've all heard the same story about Spielberg. Second, and more important, today's film studios are run differently from those of the 1970s. More security and less access.

What's valuable about role models is not the strategies they pursued, but the thought processes that led them to those strategies. It's those ways of thinking, channeled through today's realities, that will create the approach you'll need to land your dream job.

Spielberg, for example, had an almost megalomaniacal belief in his ability to make good films, and a complete imperviousness to the opinions of others about his talent. (He was rejected from film school twice.)

Anyone whose dream job is that of film director would definitely need to think that way, but the strategy necessary to create that career today would more likely involve posting Internet fan films than a studio internship.

3. BE WILLING TO PAY THE PRICE.

You can do anything, but you can't do everything. If you're going to pursue your dream job—and absolutely succeed at achieving it—you *may* need to sacrifice other things, such as having a family, or eating regularly.

I emphasize the word *may* because that sacrifice is not always required. Plenty of people have their dream jobs and still manage to spend time with their families, pursue hobbies, and so forth. (I'm one of them.)

While you might not be called on to make huge sacrifices to achieve your dream job, you must be *willing* to do so.

Hopefully you'll be able to get to where you want to be without having to give up the other things you value. However, if you're not willing to give them up, you'll never reach your goal, because you won't take the necessary risks.

4. LEARN TO SELL.

No matter what your dream job might be, you're not going to get it unless you learn how to sell. I'm not saying you need to be a professional salesperson. However, if you can't sell, you can't sell yourself or your ideas.

For example, suppose your dream job is being a high-tech CEO. You may have the most innovative idea since automatic bread-slicing, but if you can't sell that idea, you won't attract investors, customers, or talented employees.

Knowing how to sell yourself gives you the edge. Consider this: a mediocre performer who knows how to sell *always* beats an exceptional performer who doesn't. And an exceptional performer who also knows how to sell is virtually unbeatable.

Finding a great job always involves selling yourself and your skills. And being successful at any career means constantly selling the value of the services you're providing. For example, Picasso was a brilliant artist, but he was equally brilliant at self-promotion.

5. CREATE A PLAN AND TAKE MASSIVE ACTION.

Every "success formula" starts with (1) knowing where you are today, (2) knowing where you want to be, and (3) building a plan to get from here to there. Now you need a plan. Create one.

That plan may involve meeting new people, doing new things, learning new things...the specifics of the plan are going to vary according to who you are, where you are, and where you want to get.

Even if you've been serious about Step 2 of this method and trained yourself to think like your role models, your plan won't be perfect, and chances are, it's not going to work...at least not all of it.

However, you can't let that keep you from taking action. In fact, you want to take as much action as possible so you learn as quickly as possible which parts of your plan are going to work and which need adjustment.

The sad truth is that even when people have plans, they don't take enough action. Tentative steps simply aren't good. Where the normal person would do a couple of actions to make the plan real, you should do twenty. Or thirty.

For example, I recently met two men whose dream job was to write science fiction for a living. Both were equally talented, but one sent his manuscript to a single small publisher and waited for six months. The other sent his manuscript to a dozen small presses and a dozen agents.

Guess which of these two writers is now a published author.

6. ADJUST YOUR PLAN BASED ON RESULTS.

Taking massive action makes it impossible to fool yourself into thinking that the reason you didn't get your dream job is that you didn't try hard enough. Massive action forces you to reevaluate your plan if you don't get where you want to be.

In other words, your results allow you to go back and build another, more refined, plan based on your hard-won experience. Now that you're armed with valuable knowledge of what didn't work, your new plan will be far more likely to succeed.

If you truly believe, in your gut, that your dream job is right for you, and truly believe that you're willing to do whatever it takes to get that job, you'll find a way to get it. It's truly that simple.

You may also find that your dream evolves and changes as you learn. You might even land your dream job and then decide that it's not really what you expected or really want to do.

So even though you need to be focused, it never hurts to explore more than one area of interest, if only to diversify your skills.

For example, at one time my dream job was that of playing rock and roll professionally. I have absolutely no interest in that career path now, but my pursuit of that goal in my young adulthood taught me valuable lessons about stage presence, how to sell services, and how to build a team that can play well together. Each of those skills has stood me in good stead at some point in my career.

SHORTCUT

DREAM JOBS

- **KNOW** what would constitute your dream job.
- **FIND** role models and incorporate their way of thinking.
- **HAVE** the courage to sacrifice your security.
- **ESSENTIAL:** learn to sell.
- **CREATE** a plan and start executing it today.
- **ADJUST** your plan as you learn more about yourself.

25

How to Land a Job Interview

Getting a job interview is a classic sales situation. Your goal is to match what you've got to offer to the needs of the customer (the hiring firm). Here's how:

1. IF POSSIBLE, CREATE YOUR OWN JOB DESCRIPTION.

The best job interviews always result from your figuring out, on your own, how you can help a company get new customers, break into new markets, or reduce costs.

To do this, use the Internet to research your target company, its customers, and its competitors. If possible, contact individuals in the target company in order to better understand what they might be seeking.

However, let's suppose that you're applying for a preexisting job opening that's described on a website. The subsequent steps will increase the likelihood that you'll get an interview.

2. IF POSSIBLE, GET A REFERRAL.

Your goal is to land an interview with the real decision-maker, the person for whom you'll eventually be working. You're more likely to achieve that goal if you can bypass the gatekeepers (usually Human Resources).

Therefore, if you've got contacts inside a company, and those contacts know you and trust you, ask them to reach out to the decision-maker and recommend you personally.

In other words, resort to a résumé only when it's the only way to get an interview. In *all* other cases you're better off crafting a specific letter, or e-mail, to a specific person and otherwise pursuing him or her directly.

3. REWRITE YOUR RÉSUMÉ FOR EACH JOB.

The purpose of a résumé is to present the history of your education and employment so potential employers can assess whether to hire you, right? Wrong! A résumé is a sales document that helps an employer understand whether interviewing you makes sense.

A potential employer doesn't really care what you did or where you did it. All a prospective employer cares about is *what you can do for his or her company* now and in the future. Therefore, like all sales documents, your résumé is *about the customer, not about you.* I can't emphasize this point strongly enough.

Some people think that the way to get a hiring company interested is to attach a customized cover letter to a general-purpose résumé. There's a word for these people: *unemployed.*

How many times have you heard somebody say, "I've sent out hundreds of résumés and haven't gotten a single interview"? This complaint is common because general-purpose résumés are highly unlikely to match what a potential employer is looking for.

Your résumé is far more likely to make it through first-pass screening and cause a hiring manager to read it and call you if it's customized specifically for the hiring company and the job that it's seeking to fill.

4. MODEL YOUR "WHO I AM" ON THE JOB DESCRIPTION.

HR groups (and the résumé-screening programs they use) automatically bypass résumés that don't match the job description. Therefore, in order to pass the first screening, your résumé must echo the terminology that's in the ad.

For example, suppose an ad reads as follows:

> ABC Software would like to invite ambitious, hard-working individuals to apply for the position of full-time outside sales. Applicants should be able to bring new ideas and improvements to business practices; remain fair, respectful, and moral in all situations; and work well both independently and as part of a team.

In this case, the first line of your résumé (right after your name) should read something like this:

> An ambitious, hard-working, moral individual, looking for a full-time job in outside sales, with the opportunity to work both independently and as part of a team.

This isn't pandering. Many companies routinely use résumé search software that filters out those that don't contain the right "magic words."

5. STATE BENEFITS RATHER THAN HISTORY.

What's important in a résumé isn't the jobs you've held, but how the value you've provided your other employers in the past (or your educational experience) will translate into value to the hiring firm. Example:

WRONG:

> 2002–2007. Line manager at Acme. Supervised ten employees on a widget manufacturing line. Won "best quality" award.

RIGHT:

Increased widget production by 25 percent at Acme by instituting an award-winning quality control program.

6. HIT ALL THE HOT BUTTONS.

Go through the job description and isolate the elements that the hiring firm thinks are important. Then write benefits statements, based on your experience and education, that match as many of these elements as possible.

If you are plainly and obviously unqualified for the job (e.g., it asks for five years of experience and you're just out of school), don't waste your time sending a résumé. You won't get the job unless you already know somebody at the hiring firm or develop contacts that can provide you an introduction to the hiring manager.

SHORTCUT

LANDING AN INTERVIEW

- **IF** possible, create and sell your own job description.
- **IF** possible, get a current employee to recommend you.
- **CUSTOMIZE** your résumé to match the job description.
- **EXPLAIN** "who I am" in terms of the specific job.
- **DESCRIBE** specifically how you helped former employers.
- **INCLUDE** benefits that echo phrases from the job description.

How to Ace a Job Interview

Most people get flustered at even the idea of a job interview. On the one hand they're trying to get hired, and on the other hand they're often struggling with emotions: preparing for disappointment or wondering whether they'll really be happy if they get the job.

The following method gets you out of that state and into a state where the job interview can actually be enjoyable:

1. HAVE OTHER OPTIONS.

When you're up for a job interview, the natural impulse is to focus entirely on that interview, rather than on your ongoing job search. This is a huge mistake, because the last thing you want is the desperate feeling that you must get this job.

The moment you get a job interview, you should step up your job search so you have additional options. Rather than limit yourself to this one interview, use the fact that you've gotten it to create the confidence that will win you more interviews.

2. RESEARCH THE HIRING FIRM.

Unless this interview dropped into your lap by accident (rarely the case), chances are that you've already done some research into the hiring firm to get yourself on the interview list. It's now time to step up your research efforts.

Search out and memorize the names of the key executives in the area where you're likely to be interviewing, as well as some facts about their careers. If possible, use your social networking contacts to interview people who can give you an insider's perspective.

Acquire a working knowledge of the hiring firm's industry and the firm's largest customers. If the firm is publicly held, review the firm's latest 10-Q report on SEC.gov. Search for recent business news stories. LinkedIn is also useful because the more you learn about the "players" in the hiring firm, the better you'll be able to position your services.

3. PREPARE INSIGHTFUL QUESTIONS.

It's a common mistake to assume that a job interview means you're just being interviewed for the job. That's only half of the truth. You're also interviewing the firm, and the people in it, to decide whether that firm is a good match *for you*.

Based on your research, craft three questions that will help you clarify how you can best contribute to the success of the hiring firm. For example, if you're a programmer with Unix experience, you might ask about the company's specific usage of Unix.

Such questions are also intended to start conversations that can help the hiring manager see why you'd be valuable. Needless to say, these should not be questions about what the hiring firm can do for you but lead toward a discussion of how you can help the company.

WRONG:

- "What kind of vacation plan do you have?"
- "Does the health plan include dental coverage?"

RIGHT:

- "I understand that you're thinking of expanding sales into the automotive industry. From your perspective, how could my experience in consumer electronic marketing help you succeed in that industry?"
- "Beyond what's obvious from the job description, what are the most important attributes needed to be successful in this environment?"

4. REHEARSE THE OBVIOUS ANSWERS.

Many job interviewers feel obligated to ask entirely predictable job interview questions (such as "What's your greatest strength?"). There are dozens of websites that can help you prepare for these questions. Read them and rehearse your answers.

A word of warning here: companies with interviewers who ask these pat questions tend to be old-fashioned and bureaucratic. Such questions are therefore a warning that, unless you can tolerate unimaginativeness, you might be better off working elsewhere.

In general, all of these questions are opportunities for you to present whatever experience you have in the context of how you can apply that experience to help the hiring firm satisfy a need, avoid a risk, or take advantage of an opportunity.

Two quick words of warning:

1. Never say anything negative about a former employer, even if your bosses were a collection of prime jerks. I once saw a résumé that was a list of complaints about the "idiots" the job seeker had worked for. Needless to say, he never got a job offer.

2. If you're forced to state your salary requirements, give a wide range and make it clear that you understand the range is dependent

on the actual responsibilities of the job. Ideally you want *them* to make the first offer.

5. DRESS APPROPRIATELY AND ARRIVE EARLY.

Dress the same as the *managers* where you're interviewing. For example, if you're a man interviewing at a high-tech firm in California, wear a clean pair of Dockers, a high-quality golf shirt, and expensive running shoes. Wear a suit and you'll look like a dork.

Conversely, if you're interviewing at a financial services firm in New York City, you're more likely to land the job if you're wearing a suit that looks as if it cost a thousand dollars, even if you're applying for an entry-level position.

If you don't know what's appropriate, ask somebody who works there. If that's not practical, try to scout the place out beforehand. Find an inconspicuous place around the entrance or the parking lot and notice how people dress.

The trick to arriving early (but not too early) is to leave for your appointment with at least an hour to spare. Once you're in the general geographical area, find somewhere comfortable to wait and relax, then show up ten minutes early.

All of the steps above are designed to increase your comfort level with the interview process so you don't come off as desperate (which is the kiss of death).

As you enter the interview, think of yourself as being in a position to learn something: about the company, about the people in it, and even about yourself. Curiosity is the "power emotion" in all sales situations, but especially when you're selling yourself.

6. FOLLOW THROUGH, THEN DECIDE.

After the interview, send an e-mail thanking the people who interviewed you. Be positive about the experience, but don't gush. You want the hiring firm to think you're doing it a favor by accepting a job, not that it's doing you a favor by offering you one.

After you've interviewed, you might not feel entirely certain that you actually want that job. Ignore that feeling, because it may be your emotions setting you up to not feel disappointed if you don't get it.

Instead, play out the hand and worry about whether you want the job after you've gotten the offer. Meanwhile, continue your job search, secure in the fact that, at the very least, you've honed your interview skills.

SHORTCUT

JOB INTERVIEWS

- **DON'T** have all your eggs in this one basket.
- **FIND** out all you can about the hiring firm.
- **DEVISE** questions that show you've done your research.
- **REHEARSE** answers to the standard questions.
- **WEAR** what you'd wear if you worked there; don't be late.
- **GET** the offer, then decide whether you really want the job.

SECRET **27**

How to Make Failure
Impossible

In my opinion too much has been written about how to be successful, so instead I'm going to show you how to set things up in your
brain so it's impossible for you to fail. Here's how:

1. SET ACHIEVABLE YET INSPIRATIONAL GOALS.

If you don't believe your goal is achievable, you won't take action to
achieve it. Therefore, any goal that you set must be within the realm
of possibility and tied to actions that you can actually take.

A goal must also be inspirational enough to motivate you to take
action. For example, "Lose some weight" is achievable but not particularly inspirational. "Reach and maintain my ideal weight of 170
pounds" is both achievable and motivating.

As a general rule, big goals are more inspirational than small
ones, provided they're not so big that (in your heart of hearts) you
don't believe you can achieve them. That being said, most people are
far more capable of success than they suspect.

2. WRITE THEM DOWN SO THEY MOTIVATE.

Talk is cheap and goals aren't real unless they're written down. And
by "written down," I don't mean typed on a computer or tablet. I

mean written by you using your hand to move a pen (not a pencil) around on a piece of paper.

Taking time to actually form the letters (rather than just tapping a piece of plastic) subliminally tells your mind that these goals are important and different and not a text e-mail that you're sending to yourself, soon composed and soon forgotten.

Also, write your goals down more than once. In fact, write them down as many times as you can manage.

To give extra oomph to your efforts, make a formal public commitment to your goals. For example, you might want to sign up for a charity race that you couldn't possibly run without first getting yourself in tip-top shape.

3. DECIDE THAT YOU MUST ACHIEVE YOUR GOALS.

Once you've gotten your goals set in your mind, it's time to take action. The important thing here is to approach each action with confidence that you'll eventually succeed. To do this you must harness your internal dialogue.

When you approach a task that leads toward your goal, never start out by saying, "I'll try…" When you use that phrase, you're giving yourself permission to fail. Instead, phrase your action in terms of "I will…!" or "I must…!" No wiggle room allowed.

It's only through being 100 percent committed to taking action that you'll achieve an ambitious goal. So if you truly want to succeed, banish all thoughts of giving up. You *will* get there eventually because you *must*.

4. SET MEASURABLE MILESTONES.

Big goals are easier to achieve if you break them up into smaller chunks or milestones. Achieving milestones gives you more confidence, strengthens your motivation, and helps you build momentum.

The word *milestone* comes from a marker that measures distance on a road. The term has stood the test of time because the concept—measuring something quantifiable—is essential.

A milestone should always be something specific so you know, without any doubt, whether you've achieved it.

WRONG:

"Develop contacts in my field of expertise."

RIGHT:

"Have conversations with ten different experts in my field."

5. MONITOR YOUR PROGRESS.

Revisit your goals every day to remind yourself what's important to you. Post them on your bathroom mirror, on the background of your computer screen, and on the dashboard of your car.

Set reminders in your e-mail and calendar programs to keep you focused on achieving your goals rather than just performing activities that pop up throughout your daily life. Harness technology to focus your efforts rather than distract you.

Keep a record of what you've already accomplished. Review this when you're feeling discouraged or unsure—it's an instant confidence builder and helps you focus on the positive.

6. TREAT SETBACKS AS SIGNALS.

A setback is something that blocks you from achieving a goal. Most people treat setbacks as mini-failures, and often use them as an excuse to give up...and therefore fail.

Every successful person has encountered setbacks, but learning what doesn't work is an essential part of learning what does! Setbacks are a sign that you're making progress.

Treat setbacks as signals that you might need to change your approach to achieve the goal. If an action consistently results in a setback, consider taking a different action. Repeat as necessary.

7. REDEFINE *FAILURE* AS "FAILING TO TAKE ACTION."

This is the most important part. Indeed, the previous steps were only laying the groundwork for this one. Consider: regardless of your goals and milestones, you don't have control over anything except your own behavior.

Redefining failure as "failing to take action" puts failure (and therefore success) within your control. When the only *true* failure is inactivity, you cannot fail...as long as you continue to take action.

So what's the worst-case scenario when you think this way? It's this: you might die before you achieve your goal. But you'll still be successful because *if failure is failing to take action, you were successful the moment you took action to achieve your goal!*

SHORTCUT

TRANSCENDING FAILURE

- **CREATE** goals that motivate you to achieve something possible.

- **ALWAYS** write goals down; display them where you'll see them.

- **DECIDE** by saying "I must..." or "I will..." rather than "I'll try..."

- **BREAK** your big goals into smaller, measurable milestones.

- **CHECK** whether you're moving toward or away from your goals.

- **WELCOME** setbacks because they'll hone your plan.

- **THE** only true failure is failing to take action.

How to Become More Optimistic

If you truly want to be successful, it's in your best interest to create and maintain a positive attitude. When you've got an attitude of optimism, expectancy, and enthusiasm, opportunities grow and problems shrink. Here's how it's done:

1. BEGIN EACH DAY WITH EXPECTATION.

Your experience at work and in life generally lives up (or down) to your expectations. Therefore, when you rise from bed, make your first thought be "Something wonderful is going to happen today."

There's a big lesson here, which is that your attitude isn't controlled by events. While truly sad things do happen, most of the time your attitude is the result of how you're viewing the world, rather than what's happening in it.

It's absolutely true that the day's events might not proceed in the manner you'd prefer. Even so, if you keep looking for something positive to happen, your mind will find something that fulfills that expectation.

2. ASSUME OTHER PEOPLE MEAN WELL.

It's impossible to really know the "why" behind the "what" that people do. Attributing other people's weird behaviors to evil motives adds extra misery to life, while assuming good intentions leaves you open to reconciliation.

You can't read minds and you don't have everyone wired to a lie detector. Truly you have no idea what anyone is really thinking or why people do what they do. In most cases people are doing the best they can with the resources they've got.

Before you tell a story about somebody else (or listen to one), ask yourself four questions: (1) is it true? (2) is it kind? (3) is it necessary? and (4) would I want somebody telling a similar story about me? Treat others as you'd like to be treated.

3. AVOID DEPRESSING CONVERSATIONS.

Stop complaining about the economy, your company, or your customers. Same thing with your personal problems and illnesses. What does it do, other than depress you and everyone else around you?

Similarly, it's wasting your breath to argue about things, such as religion and politics, that get people all riled up. When such topics surface, bow out. Say something like, "Whether I agree or not, it's not a useful discussion for us to have right now."

Some battles aren't worth fighting, and many people are easier to handle when they think they've won the argument. What's important isn't "winning," but what you, and the other people involved, plan to do next.

4. LET GO OF YOUR RESULTS.

The big enemy of happiness is worry, which comes from focusing on events that are outside your control. Once you've taken action, there's usually nothing more you can do. Focus on the job at hand rather than some fantasy of what might happen.

The nature of the physical universe is change. Nothing remains the same; everything is, as the gurus say, transitory. Whether you're celebrating or mourning or something in between, this too will pass.

Remember that while some work environments are inherently difficult, if you're consistently miserable, it's your fault. You owe it to yourself and your coworkers to either find a job that makes you happy or make the best of the job you've got.

5. IMPROVE THE QUALITY OF YOUR LIFE.

Sometimes we can't avoid scarfing something quickly to keep us up and running. Even so, at least once a day, try to eat something really delicious, such as a small chunk of fine cheese or an imported chocolate. Focus on it; taste it; savor it.

In addition, many households leave their TVs on as background noise while they're doing other things. The entire point of broadcast TV is to make you dissatisfied with your life. If you want some background noise, play an audiobook.

Finally, go through your home and office and throw out *everything* that isn't useful or beautiful. Why would you want to pollute your life and your environment with objects that are useless and ugly?

6. ADOPT AN ATTITUDE OF GRATITUDE.

The small and large successes and accomplishments in your life deserve recognition. It's a mistake to move on to the next task or goal without celebrating, even if only by patting yourself on the back.

Similarly, give a verbal gift to everyone you meet—a smile, a word of encouragement, a gesture of politeness, or even a friendly nod. Always say, "Thank you," even for the smallest of services.

Finally, just before you go to bed, write down at least one wonderful thing that happened. It might be something as small as a making a child laugh or as huge as landing a million-dollar deal. Be grateful for the day, because it will never come again.

7. FOCUS ON THE FUTURE.

Focusing on past mistakes or wrongs inflicted on you is like driving a car while looking in the rearview mirror. You'll keep heading in the same direction until you collide with something solid.

While you can and should learn from the past, keep your thoughts on the future. Daydream about how things might be better. It's when you let your thoughts wander that you're more likely to have the insights that create your future.

Above all, believe that the best is yet to come. When my grandmother was in her seventies, she returned to college, traveled across Europe in youth hostels, and learned Japanese painting. The last thing she told me was, "You know, Geoffers, life begins at ninety."

SHORTCUT

BECOMING OPTIMISTIC

- **EXPECT** something wonderful to happen every day.

- **DON'T** try to read minds; treat people as you'd want to be treated.

- **DON'T** waste breath fighting about things you can't change.

- **CONCENTRATE** on the job at hand, not the results you seek.

- **TAKE** better control of the pleasures in your life.

- **BE** thankful for every day and every accomplishment, yours and others'.

- **REMEMBER** that the best is yet to come.

V

How to
Communicate

Communication isn't just important in business; it is the very core of business itself. While individual contributors may work alone, their work has no meaning unless other people know about it.

Managing is communication, selling is communication, marketing is communication. You'd think, given its importance, that business-people would be good at communicating. However, that's not usually the case.

The business world is chockablock with bloated documents, cryptic e-mails, pointless conversations, and boring meetings. Fortunately it doesn't have to be this way, as the following secrets explain:

- "Five Rules for Business Communication" contains the essential keys to making yourself understood, regardless of whether you're communicating in person, over the phone, or online.
- "How to Have a Real Conversation" describes how to fully understand what another person is trying to say and then move the conversation forward toward whatever decision you want the other person to make.

■ "How to Write a Compelling E-mail" provides the process for composing a crisp, easily read message that both helps the recipient understand the decision you want made and drives the recipient to make that decision.

■ "How to Give a Memorable Presentation" explains how to guide an audience through a set of emotions using the power of your voice and your ideas, as well as essential rules to make your presentation more effective.

■ "How to Work a Room" gives you the tools you need to build business contacts at conferences, meetings, and social events, without seeming pushy and while staying within the bounds of social convention.

■ "How to Negotiate an Agreement" contains the essence of getting what you want in return for what you're offering. This method applies to every negotiation from simple salary discussions to million-dollar sales.

■ "How to Handle Alarming E-mails" describes the three e-mails that nobody ever wants to receive and how you can respond to them in a way that both protects your interests and moves your agenda forward.

Five Rules for Business Communication

Most business communication is dreadful: fluff-filled internal e-mails, dead-boring presentations, conversations that start and end nowhere, sales messages that leave customers scratching their heads.

In every organization the real leader is whoever can communicate the most clearly and make complicated things seem simple and simple things seem obvious.

Five rules apply to *all* business communication. Learn them, memorize them, practice them, and make them part of your everyday mental toolbox.

1. PINPOINT THE PURPOSE BEHIND THE COMMUNICATION.

Communication is information with a purpose. Therefore, it's possible to communicate well only if you are clear about the purpose of the communication.

Therefore, before you initiate any communication at work, ask yourself the following three questions (and answer them):

1. What decision am I seeking?
2. Whom do I want to make this decision?
3. Is this the right time to ask that person?

The clearer your answers to these questions, the clearer your communication will be.

2. CHOOSE A MEDIUM THAT'S CONVENIENT FOR THE DECISION-MAKER.

It was famously said in the twentieth century that "the medium is the message." Now that we're all inundated with media, that's no longer true. Today you want the medium to be "transparent" so the decision-maker focuses on the decision.

Always use the medium (or media) that demands the least mental and emotional effort from the decision-maker.

For example, never ask for a face-to-face meeting if the decision you want made can be effectively handled through a quick exchange of texts or e-mails. Similarly, never use e-mail when the decision requires the personal touch of a face-to-face interaction.

For example, if you're using e-mail to avoid feeling uncomfortable (such as when delivering bad news), you're choosing a medium based on your needs rather than those of the decision-maker.

3. SIMPLIFY WORDS AND SENTENCES.

The business world is complicated enough without your using five-dollar words when five-cent ones will do the job better. Below is a real-life example, a press release selected at random (with my rewrite):

WRONG:

"Acme provides GPS intelligence for small and medium-sized businesses to track/manage/automate their mobile fleets. Based on data and metrics Acme provides, SMBs gain visibility and actionable intelligence to adjust their service vehicles accordingly for both improved customer satisfaction and bottom line."

RIGHT:

"Acme tracks the location of your service trucks so you know where they are and can get them where they need to go. This saves you money because you can now service more customers with the same-size fleet."

The original forces the decision-maker to struggle to figure out what's being sold. What does "GPS intelligence" mean? Or "track/manage/automate"? The problem is not that the original is completely indecipherable, but that it needs to be deciphered at all.

By contrast, the rewrite simply says what's being sold and why it's important to the decision-maker. I should emphasize that the original press release is better than average, though; I've read plenty that were far more convoluted.

The trick to simplifying your communication is: *write the way you talk*. In my experience almost *everybody* is better at talking clearly than at writing clearly. If you've got to write something, do this:

1. Use the "record" function on your phone, tablet, or PC.
2. Imagine yourself talking to a colleague.
3. Say whatever it is you want to say (keeping your purpose in mind).
4. Play back and transcribe what you just recorded.
5. Edit out any biz-blab or jargon that accidentally slipped in.

Once you've done this a few times, you may find that you can "hit record" in your head and hear yourself talking. Eventually it becomes automatic.

4. REPLACE BUSINESS CLICHÉS WITH PLAIN LANGUAGE.

Many businessfolk believe that their communications will seem more businesslike and profound if they pepper them with business clichés, buzzwords, and biz-blab. Such people are ~~idiots~~ mistaken.

For example, high-tech marketing documents frequently describe products as "cutting-edge," "industry-leading," "third-generation," "fourth-generation," "leading-edge," "state-of-the-art," "2.0," and "next-generation."

None of these terms mean anything. Not really. Far from making the stuff seem more exciting, biz-blab marks the person who uses it as (at best) an unoriginal thinker and (at worst) a fool.

Bulking up your communication with business clichés also slows decision-making down. Below is an example from a real-life business document, along with my rewrite:

WRONG:

> "In order to focus externally, we must focus both externally and internally (customer's customer and internal alignment necessary to respond), with internal collaboration with common focus/goals by stakeholders accountable for ultimate business results oriented, optimized and coordinated outputs, aligned around the sales cycle and with a proactive approach to higher order competency investments and being unwilling to throw deliverables over the fence to sales teams and trust results will be achieved."

RIGHT:

> "We should measure changes in sales revenue to make certain the sales training actually worked."

I could list a bunch of business buzzwords, but there are so many of them (and more are created every year) that it would be pointless. Instead I suggest you do a Web search for "list of business buzzwords." You'll find plenty to avoid.

5. REPLACE TECHNICAL JARGON WITH EVERYDAY WORDS.

This rule applies only if you're an expert attempting to communicate with a non-expert. When experts communicate with other experts, jargon is useful because it allows bursts of communication without an explanation of stuff both parties already know.

However, jargon prevents non-experts from understanding what you're talking about, which makes it difficult or impossible for them to make the decision you want. If you want non-experts on board, replace jargon with commonly understood terms.

WRONG:

> "Dielectric interference that's trivial at 24 nm will likely overload at 12 nm."

RIGHT:

> "Computer chips that contain electrical components that are smaller than 1/8000th the width of a human hair—about half the size of today's components—may not be reliable. Why? Because the electricity in those components might make them interfere with each other, as when your cell phone crackles on a call when you're standing next to a microwave."

Note that using commonly understood words usually takes longer than expressing the same thought using technical jargon. It also takes a lot more thought and effort, because you must "get outside" your expertise and imagine how a non-expert might approach and understand the subject matter. However, it's worth the extra effort if you truly want non-experts to understand you.

CLEAR BUSINESS COMMUNICATION

- **ALWAYS** know your reason for communicating.
- **PICK** a medium that's appropriate for the other person.
- **SIMPLIFY** your message for easy mental consumption.
- **EDIT** out the buzzwords and corporate-speak.
- **AVOID** jargon unless dealing with fellow experts.

30

How to Have a Real Conversation

Here's a simple four-step process for making certain that every business conversation serves your purpose, whether you're face-to-face, on the phone, or trading e-mails or texts. In the latter two cases you have a bit more time to think, but that's the only difference.

1. KNOW WHY YOU'RE HAVING THE CONVERSATION.

There are times at work when you'll just be enjoying the company of other people. While you need to be careful not to spread gossip or blurt something stupid, when you're "shooting the bull" (as they say), you can relax and have fun.

However, if you need to talk about something important, it's best not to jump into the conversation without having an explicit goal in mind. Having a goal keeps the conversation focused, preventing you from wasting time and energy.

Similarly, if somebody starts a conversation with you, it's often useful to wonder why the conversation is happening and why now. It's not worth obsessing about, but if you've got a sense of the "why" it's easier to get "where" the conversation needs to go.

2. IGNORE YOUR "MONKEY MIND."

The ancient Chinese believed everyone has a "monkey mind" that jumps from thought to thought, like so:

- What is she thinking about me?
- Will I make a sale?
- What if I can't pay the mortgage?
- Gosh, that wallpaper is ugly.
- I've got to get to the airport in two hours.
- Etc., etc., etc.

This constant mental noise pulls your attention away from whomever you're conversing with and toward your own perspectives, priorities, and goals.

If you listen to your "monkey mind," you'll hear only a percentage of what the other person is saying. In all likelihood you'll misunderstand and/or forget what was said.

You practice ignoring your monkey mind by sitting quietly by yourself and listening to it chatter away. By becoming more aware of it, you can more easily identify it and differentiate it from the focused thoughts that are relevant to a conversation.

3. ACKNOWLEDGE, RECAP, AND RESPOND.

When the other person has finished speaking, do not just leap into what you want to say next. Make some acknowledgment—even if just a nod of the head or a short "Ah!"—that you've heard the other person, rather than the chattering of your "monkey mind."

If the other person has said something complex or emotional, or has introduced significant new information, briefly recount and characterize what he or she said.

Recapping what you've heard gives the other person an opportunity to correct any misperception or to elaborate as necessary to ensure you "get it." It also prevents the conversation from going awry based on a correctible misunderstanding.

Regardless of whether you've recapped, pause for a moment to consider what you heard, and then respond with a statement, story, or question that adds to the conversation and moves it closer to its point and purpose.

For example, if a potential customer shares the details of a business problem, you might then tell a brief story—once you've restated the problem and are sure you understand it—about how another company handled a similar problem.

While the above method seems a bit artificial when first practiced, with time it becomes second nature.

SHORTCUT

MEANINGFUL CONVERSATIONS

- **KNOW** the reason you're having a conversation.
- **IGNORE** your "monkey mind."
- **CONSIDER** what was said, rephrase if necessary, respond appropriately.

SECRET **31**

How to Write a Compelling E-mail

This is a foolproof six-step method for writing an e-mail that helps convince the reader to take the action you'd prefer:

1. KNOW THE DECISION YOU WANT MADE.

E-mails are the most common form of communication in the business world. Unfortunately many are so poorly written that recipients must struggle to figure out why they are reading the e-mail and what they are supposed to do about it.

Therefore, as with any business communication, when writing an e-mail you must start by understanding exactly what decision you want made. Until you're clear on this essential point, don't send the e-mail. It'll just be a waste of time, both yours and the recipient's.

2. WRITE THE CONCLUSION FIRST.

Your conclusion is a simple statement of the decision you want the recipient to make, based on the contents of your e-mail.

In school they probably taught you to start with an introduction and end with a conclusion. Bad advice.

Nobody in the business world has time to wander through the

development of an idea. If you don't tell people the reason for the e-mail immediately, chances are they'll just move on.

So start with your conclusion. For example, suppose your goal is to get your boss to approve an in-house gym.

WRONG:

> Jim,
>
> As you know, employee absenteeism is generally recognized as an ongoing problem with a steep financial impact, both in our company and in other companies in our industry. [Yada, yada, yada.] Therefore, we should consider allocating money for the installation of a gym at our headquarter facility.

RIGHT:

> Jim,
>
> I want you to approve the installation of an in-house gym.

Note that the "right" way simply gets to the point without all the excess verbiage.

3. STRUCTURE ARGUMENTS INTO DIGESTIBLE CHUNKS.

Once you've stated your conclusion (i.e., the decision you want made), collect the arguments that support it. To make your arguments "digestible," break them into small chunks, presenting each point with a similar format and sentence structure.

WRONG:

> According to a recently published government report, group physical fitness is extremely

important even though very few companies actually
demonstrate a commitment to it! Many firms identify
physical fitness as an undervalued competitive
asset, but don't have a plan for improvement in
this area, even though physical fitness is strongly
linked to corporate and individual economic and
personal success. I feel that if we do not address
the issue of physical fitness as it enhances
workplace productivity, we will be left behind.

RIGHT:

An in-house gym will:
- Reduce absenteeism
- Increase overall productivity

Once again, the "right" way hits the most important points without wasting time on extraneous issues.

4. BOLSTER EACH ARGUMENT WITH EVIDENCE.

A "statement of fact" is only an opinion unless you can prove that the statement is actually a fact. While your opinion may influence those who trust you, most of the time you'll want evidence to back it up. The best evidence comes from quoting an authoritative source.

WRONG:

An in-house gym will reduce absenteeism because
people will want to come to work rather than stay
at home since they'll have more energy and they
won't get sick so much.

RIGHT:

- Reduce absenteeism. Companies with in-house gyms experience 20 percent less absenteeism than those that lack them, according to the National Health Institute.

The "right" example expands one of the arguments with a verifiable fact. Do the same with any other arguments you make.

5. REPEAT YOUR CONCLUSION AS A CALL TO ACTION.

At the end of the e-mail, restate the conclusion in a way that provides the recipient with the next step he or she must take—assuming you've convinced that person to support the decision. Keep it simple and specific.

WRONG:

Your support for this project would be greatly appreciated.

RIGHT:

When you respond to this e-mail with your approval, I'll get the process started.

6. INSERT A BENEFIT IN THE SUBJECT LINE.

Your subject line (aka the title) is the most important part of your e-mail, because your choice of words determines whether the e-mail gets opened and read. That's why you write it last, after you've written down both your conclusion and the arguments and evidence that support it.

Ideally a subject line should do two things: (1) create enough interest or curiosity that the recipient opens and reads the e-mail, and (2) imply the conclusion that you want the recipient to accept (i.e., the decision you want made).

In most cases the best way to accomplish both tasks is to encapsulate a benefit (or benefits) that will result from the decision you'd like the recipient to make.

WRONG:

> To: Jim@Acme.com
> Subject: The Health Impact of In-House Employee Fitness Programs

RIGHT:

> To: Jim@Acme.com
> Subject: How we can reduce absenteeism

Note that the "right" example positions the e-mail as something that requires action, while the "wrong" example positions the e-mail as a theoretical discussion.

SHORTCUT

WRITING E-MAILS

- **KNOW** what decision you want made.
- **FIRST** express that decision as a conclusion.
- **SUPPORT** that conclusion with simple arguments.
- **PROVIDE** evidence to bolster each argument.
- **REPEAT** your conclusion as an action item.
- **WRITE** the subject last and include a benefit.

SECRET **32**

How to Give a Memorable Presentation

Most business presentations consist of bullet-pointed outlines interspersed with illustrations (tables and graphics). Sometimes these outlines contain notes, usually intended for the speaker, but possibly including detailed information about individual slides.

The best presentations, however, are those in which the focus is on the speaker and what he or she has to say, while the slides play a supporting role. Here's how to create not only a presentation that people will remember, but one that will convince them to take action:

1. REDUCE YOUR STAGE FRIGHT.

The worst presentations always consist of the presenter reading his or her slides. People do this because (1) they don't know any better and (2) they've got stage fright. If you're afraid, it's only natural to cling to something predictable.

Stage fright is nothing to be sneezed at. According to at least one survey, more people are afraid of public speaking than are afraid of dying. Even so, it can be harnessed, just like any fear. (See "Secret 41. What to Do If You're Fearful.")

In addition to that method, there is a secret way to reduce stage fright. Select one person in the audience and speak directly to that person. Pretend that everyone else is just overhearing what you're saying, as at a party.

Every time you move to another part of the presentation, switch to a new person. Talking to one person not only reduces stage fright, it also makes each person in the audience feel as if you were talking to him or her personally, even if you only "target" a few people.

If you're still suffering from stage fright, I've met several people who've overcome it by joining Toastmasters International. It's easier to work through your fright when you're not speaking in front of people with whom you work.

2. CHART OUT THE EMOTIONAL JOURNEY.

The primary purpose of a presentation is not to convey information but to bring the audience from where they are now (skeptical, bored, excited, etc.) to where you'd like them to be—convinced that the decision you want made is the right one.

In other words, a presentation (i.e., the live speech) is a journey during which the audience goes from one state to another. You therefore want to structure that journey as a series of emotions, rather than a series of facts. For example:

1. Fearful. (Draw their attention to a problem.)
2. Relieved. (There is a solution to that problem.)
3. Trusting. (They believe that you and your firm are credible.)
4. Convinced. (They're ready to take action.)

Here's another structure:

1. Amazed. (Draw their attention with something they didn't know.)
2. Curious. (They see why your idea is interesting.)

3. Inspired. (They see why your idea is revolutionary.)
4. Activated. (They're now crazy anxious to buy your book.)

3. CREATE "SIGNPOST SLIDES" FOR THAT JOURNEY.

In real-world journeys, there are two types of signposts: the ones that guide you to your destination ("Smallville, Exit 9, 3 Miles") and the ones that tell you when you've arrived ("Welcome to Smallville!").

Now that you're clear on where you want to take the audience, decide which fact, graphic, or table will best serve to either head the audience in the direction in which you want them to go, or mark that they've arrived at one of the emotional way stations.

For example, suppose you're attempting to sell a solution to a particular customer problem, and your map of the emotional journey looks something like this:

1. Aware. (A problem exists.)
2. Afraid. (It's a really serious problem.)
3. Terrified. (Holy crap, we're screwed.)
4. Relieved. (Whew! Other firms have survived this.)
5. Secure. (This solution will solve the problem.)
6. Excited. (This solution might even *make* us money.)
7. Convinced. (We'd be crazy not to buy this solution.)

The signpost for "aware" might be a single slide stating a dollar number, such as an estimate of how much money is being lost because the solution is not in place.

The signposts for "afraid" might be a quote from an auditor's report and a graph showing trends in the firm's profits.

The signpost for "terrified" might be a photograph of the corporate headquarters of a firm that went out of business because it ignored warning signs.

The signpost for "relieved" might be a photograph of the corporate headquarters of a company that weathered a similar change.

While these signposts are important to the presentation, they are *not* the presentation itself. They are what's on the screen while you're giving the presentation, emphasizing and crystallizing the emotional point you're trying to make.

4. BUILD A STORY FOR EACH SIGNPOST.

Here's the big secret about great presentations: they're always a collection of stories. A story might be something as short as an explanation of how you arrived at a particular statistic, or an entire five-minute-long business anecdote.

Because stories speak to our common humanity, they are more likely to create the emotional response you're seeking.

Here's a simplified example of how the steps described so far may be implemented. In this case a person named Stan has invited John Doe to present an inventory control solution to Acme:

Emotion	Signpost Slide	Story Notes
Curious	Solving Inventory Problems at Acme John Doe, ABC Software	Stan: I've asked John to talk about inventory control. He's a solutions consultant at ABC with extensive experience in our industry. John?
Afraid	Lost Revenue = $1,000,000	John: Yes, that's a million dollars. Stan and I got together and ran the numbers and here's what we believe you're currently losing each year. If you notice in this chart, the revenue dips every time an order comes in, illustrating the overall problem.
Relieved	[Diagram showing solution]	"What we're proposing is the introduction of a new system that changes the way you handle the problem. Let me walk you through the basics..."

Emotion	Signpost Slide	Story Notes
Trusting	[Chart of company that went through a similar recovery]	"We know this is going to work because we've had experience in a similar situation. Let me tell you a story. A while back... [anecdote]."
Hopeful	[Graph showing full ROI in three months]	"Based on the expected costs, we believe you can achieve full ROI on this project within three months. Let me walk you though the process that we used to come up with this figure..."
Curious	Questions?	"Are there any questions about what we've covered so far?"
Convinced	[Schedule showing installation times]	"With your go-ahead on this project, we can have your new inventory control system up and running within six months."

The structure of the journey will of course vary, depending on the destination. The signposts may also include additional details, evidence, and examples.

5. SIMPLIFY YOUR SLIDE DECK.

When preparing your slides:

- *Keep the information relevant.* Audiences pay attention only to stories and ideas that are immediately relevant. Consider what decision you want them to make and then build an appropriate case.
- *Keep it short and sweet.* When was the last time you heard someone complain that a presentation was too short? Make it half as long as you originally thought it should be (or even shorter).
- *Use facts, not generalities.* Fuzzy concepts reflect fuzzy thinking. As with your e-mail, buttress your opinions with facts that are quantifiable, verifiable, memorable, and dramatic.

- *Simplify your graphics.* People shut off their brains when confronted with complicated drawings and tables. Use simple graphics and highlight the data points that are important.

- *Keep backgrounds in the background.* Fancy slide backgrounds only make it more difficult for you to keep the audience focused. Use a single neutral color for the background.

- *Use readable fonts.* Don't give your audience an eyestrain headache by using tiny fonts. Use large fonts in simple faces (like Arial). For added readability avoid **boldface**, *italics*, and ALL CAPS.

- *Don't get too fancy.* You want your audience to remember your message, not how many special effects you used. Remember that if your slides are attention-grabbing (as slides, not because of content), they distract from your message.

- *Adjust your presentation to the audience.* As with every business communication, use the vernacular rather than jargon and acronyms if the people in the room are not experts.

- *Rehearse your presentation.* Practice makes—well, if not perfect, at least a lot better than no practice. Rehearsing also helps you check your timing, so you don't go on too long.

6. FOLLOW THESE RULES WHEN PRESENTING.

When giving your presentation:

- *DO have a separate handout.* If there is data that you want the audience to have, put it into a separate document for distribution after your presentation. Don't use your slide deck as a data repository.

- *DO stand up rather than remaining seated.* The body language of standing while others sit keeps the focus on you and your ideas. If you're sitting with everyone else, it's a conversation, not a presentation, which is entirely different.

- *DO check your equipment in advance.* If you must use PowerPoint, or plan on showing videos or something, check to make sure the equipment really works. Then check it again. Then one more time.

- *DO have somebody else introduce you.* Write a short (one-hundred-word) bio and a short statement (fifty words) of what you'll be talking about. Have the person who invited you to the meeting read it aloud, or have it included in the invite.

- *DO set a time limit.* Since you're asking people to be a captive audience, it's only fair for you to let them know how long they are going to be captive. (This also encourages you to be brief.)

- *DON'T tell a "warm-up" joke.* Unless you're naturally humorous, telling a joke communicates that you are nervous and unsure of yourself. Leave comedy to the professionals.

- *DO take the room's "temperature."* If the group is small, have each person state what he or she would like to learn from your presentation. If the group is large, ask a question that demands a show of hands.

- *DO speak to the audience.* Great public speakers keep their focus on the audience, not on their notes. Focusing on the audience encourages the audience to focus on you and your message.

- *DON'T meander and skip.* Letting yourself digress or flip around from slide to slide simply makes you look unprepared. If you must improvise, do so within the structure of the presentation.

- *DON'T direct your remarks solely to the senior attendee.* While he or she may be the final decision-maker, it's likely that you will have to convince the others in the room to do business with you and your company as well.

- *DO make eye contact with multiple people.* As you make a point, look at one person in the audience, then continue. When you make your next point, look at a different person, and so on.

MEMORABLE PRESENTATIONS

- **TO** lessen stage fright, speak to individuals not the entire audience.

- **PLAN** out an emotional journey for the audience.

- **FLAG** the places where the audience will feel emotions.

- **BUILD** a story that creates the emotions in that order.

- **ARRANGE** everything into a simple structure.

- **MAKE** slides relevant, short, simple, and readable.

- **CUSTOMIZE** your presentation and rehearse it.

33

How to Work a Room

Even if you're naturally gregarious, it's easy to be daunted by a roomful of people you don't know, especially if those people are executives, leaders, and decision-makers you'd like to cultivate as contacts or customers.

The following process helps you circulate around a room and quickly build as many useful connections as possible:

1. BE CURIOUS ABOUT PEOPLE YOU MEET.

Whether you introduce yourself or get an introduction from somebody else, your priority is to feel and express genuine interest in the person you've just met. Ask them about themselves, why they're attending, or what they're learning.

This will almost always lead to a discussion of the other person's job or career, as well as who the other person knows. This is important information because it gives you the first indication of whether the person you've met is potentially a valuable contact.

If not, enjoy the conversation, but don't get "captured." Find an excuse to break away or talk to somebody else. The idea is to circulate so you meet more people.

2. POSITION YOURSELF IN A SINGLE SENTENCE.

If you decide to remain in the conversation, the next subject that normally comes up will be what you do for a living. This is your opportunity to position what you're offering and to begin assessing whether the other person is a potential employer.

Rather than give your job title or history, provide a description of the benefits your customers, investors, or employers get as the result of buying from, investing in, or hiring you. Ideally these benefits should include an intriguing fact.

WRONG:

- "I sell state-of-the-art training software."
- "We renegotiate IT contracts that save money."
- "I'm looking for a job in computer-game programming."

RIGHT:

- "Retail firms used the software I programmed to train employees, which increased their sales by about ten percent."
- "I helped a company lower its IT procurement costs by negotiating directly with major IT vendors."
- "I've got an idea for a computer game that combines social networking with cooperative puzzle solving."

Don't go into vast detail about yourself, the jobs you've held, or the job you want. Offer a single intriguing sentence that fits into the context of a normal conversation. You have about five to ten seconds to impress. Use them wisely.

3. OBSERVE AND LISTEN.

By positioning yourself casually yet precisely, you've given the other person the opportunity to express interest in what you just said.

If the other person stares at you blankly or changes the subject, you know that this is not a great connection for you to make, at least not now. This is a very good thing to know, because then you won't waste time trying to develop it further.

If the other person *is* interested, he or she will move the conversation to the next level by saying something like, "Wow! How do you do that?" or "Funny you should say that, we've been having problems with [something related to what you just said]."

Between these extremes is what might be called a "sliding scale" of interest. Your challenge is to figure out if the other person's interest level is high enough for you to continue the conversation.

To do this, don't just listen to what the other person says, but also observe the other person's facial expression and body language. If you sense that there's real interest (as opposed to polite interest), move to the next step.

If not, let the matter drop. Trade a few words of chitchat (e.g., "Great conference, eh?") and then extract yourself from the conversation (e.g., "Excuse me, there's somebody over there I've been meaning to catch up with.").

4. DIFFERENTIATE YOURSELF.

If, based on your one-sentence positioning, the person you've met has shown some interest in you and what you do, you now demonstrate why you're a uniquely valuable resource.

Casually reveal one or two facts about yourself that show how you're different from the competition (other people) in a way that might be interesting or essential to that person's company.

As with your initial statement, what you want is a single sentence that expresses your uniqueness using easily understood words and phrases. Examples:

- "At MIT I created a study that revealed how retail sales clerks can use past purchases to help customers take advantage of what's available in the store."
- "I've worked with so many IT vendors in the past that I know how to negotiate with them to get the best price."
- "I've used existing multiplayer game environments to test how well people can work together to solve complex problems."

5. OBSERVE AND LISTEN (AGAIN).

This is the same as Step 3. If the other person continues to show interest, move to the next step. If the other person seems disinterested or only politely interested, let the matter drop. Trade a few words of chitchat and then extract yourself from the conversation.

6. OPEN A CONVERSATION.

If there are still signs of interest, ask an open-ended question that assesses the depth and quality of the other person's interest. Examples:

- "Just out of curiosity, how does your current point-of-sale system help your people sell more?"
- "I'm curious about something. How does your firm currently negotiate with your IT vendors?"
- "You seem intrigued by my idea. What kind of games is your company looking to publish in the near future?"

No need to get fancy: just be certain the question is open-ended rather than something that can be answered with a single word. The idea is to get a conversation started, so you can ask for an appointment to pursue the matter further, outside the context of the crowd.

7. ASK FOR A REAL MEETING.

Based on the other person's response to your query, you'll know whether it makes sense to pursue the relationship. If there *is* a match between what you're offering and what the other person needs, set up a meeting to discuss the matter further:

- "What are your thoughts about having a meeting to discuss this further?"
- "It sounds like we should talk more about this. How does your calendar look?"
- "What's the best way to get on your calendar?"

If the other person agrees, trade your contact information (if this has not happened already) and make a note of the commitment so you can follow up later.

Note that the entire process takes just a few minutes and has two "exit points" to ensure you're not barking up the wrong tree. The brevity of the approach makes it easy for you to "work a room" and uncover as many potential contacts as possible.

WORKING A ROOM

- **BE** curious about people and what they do.

- **DESCRIBE** yourself in terms of the value you provide.

- **IF** the other person seems uninterested, move on.

- **EXPLAIN** how you're different from the competition.

- **IF** the other person seems uninterested, move on.

- **OPEN** a conversation to assess mutual needs.

- **IF** interest continues, ask for a real meeting.

How to Negotiate an Agreement

Negotiation consists of a back-and-forth conversation in which multiple potential decisions are proposed and discussed and a final decision agreed upon. Many negotiations are informal, but they follow the same principles as the formal negotiations described below.

Negotiations take place everywhere in business; your ability to negotiate will in many cases determine whether you'll be able to get what you want from bosses, coworkers, and customers.

1. DEFINE THE PARAMETERS.

Before you negotiate, think through what's really being negotiated.

Every business negotiation involves two elements: what's off the table and what's on the table. In addition, everything that's on the table has a maximum (the best you can expect) and a minimum (the least you'll accept).

Any part of a potential deal about which you have no flexibility whatsoever is, by definition, off the table. For example, if you're negotiating a new job but not willing to relocate, relocation is off the table.

For everything that's on the table (i.e., negotiable), figure out what the *best you can expect* and the *least you will accept* are. For example, if you're negotiating a salary, your sweetheart deal might be $150,000 a year and your bare minimum $75,000.

2. RANK THE IMPORTANCE OF WHAT IS NEGOTIABLE.

Do not negotiate until you've ranked the items identified in Step 1 in order of importance to you and possible importance to the other person. Use a scale of 1 (very important) to 3 (unimportant).

For example, if you're negotiating to hire someone, you might not really care what job title the job candidate ends up with, but it may be of great importance to the new hire. Or vice versa.

You'll be adjusting your imagined ranking for the other person as you learn more throughout the negotiation. It's possible that you'll adjust your own ranking too, if the other person brings up some compelling arguments.

3. CREATE ARGUMENTS THAT SUPPORT YOUR POSITION.

Find a reason your maximums and minimums make business sense to the other person. Usually these two points will have very different arguments behind them.

For example, suppose you expect to be paid more than other people with your education level and experience. To defend your higher salary, you might point out that you've got specialized knowledge that increases your value to the company.

On the other hand, suppose you're offered a job title that has less prestige than you expected. Your argument in this case might be "I may find it hard to do my job with a title that implies I have insufficient authority."

4. HAVE A VIABLE ALTERNATIVE.

You're at a negotiating disadvantage if you *must* close a deal and the other person only *wants* to close a deal.

For example, suppose you're trying to negotiate a final contract, and if it doesn't go through today you'll lose your job and default on your loans. Meanwhile your counterpart has no particular reason to complete the negotiations quickly. Under these circumstances you'll probably make any concession your counterpart asks for!

That's why, if at all possible, you've got to have a plan B. For example, if you're in the process of negotiating the specifics for a job that you've been offered, you should keep looking for another and even have other interviews lined up.

Keep your plan B (and your importance ranking, for that matter) from the other person. Though you might end up blurting out your plan B as a last-ditch effort, the plan is mostly to keep you from feeling desperate, and then acting from that place of desperation.

5. LET THE OTHER PERSON MAKE THE FIRST MOVE.

It's almost always to your advantage to let the other person start the negotiation process. For example, I have more than once been offered compensation for my writing that was several times what I would have asked for had I gone first.

If you get trapped into going first, present something around your maximum (for some element that's important to you), along with your argument for why it's reasonable. Be sure to leave some wiggle room for further negotiation.

WRONG:

"I charge a thousand dollars a day."

RIGHT:

"Most of my clients pay me around a thousand dollars a day for this type of work, but the actual figure depends on other elements of the agreement, such as the extent of the work involved."

6. TURN POSITIONS INTO PROBLEMS.

When you use expressions such as "my position is" or "my firm's position is," you're taking ownership of a position. This makes the position part of your identity, which makes it difficult to change or abandon it.

Rather than owning a position, externalize it into a problem that both of you are working to solve. For example: "If we crafted the arrangement like so, [idea], it would work for me. How would that work for you?"

The aim is to turn the negotiation into a problem-solving session in which you help each other figure out how to go forward... rather than butt heads.

7. ADAPT THE DEAL TO WHAT'S IMPORTANT.

In Step 2 you ranked what's important to you and to the other person. During the negotiation process, your goal is to remain flexible in order to stay true to the things that matter to you.

For example, suppose you're selling a complex software system and know that your installation team is idle right now. It's important for you to get the team working (and generating money) as soon as possible.

During the discussion you discover that it's important to the customer that he or she get the project started quickly. It should therefore be advantageous to both of you to cut the deal quickly and get everything rolling immediately.

Even when you enter negotiations with the best of intentions, it's fair to assume that at some level your counterpart wants to see you "lose" at least something. However, a part of you probably feels the same way about him or her.

So don't take it personally if your counterpart assumes negotiating positions that don't make much sense to you. Instead, let your counterpart know that every concession is meaningful and that holding out will *not* result in big rewards.

8. KNOW WHEN THE NEGOTIATION IS OVER.

If the negotiation is going well and you've got most of what you want, don't keep negotiating. If you're 90 percent there, you're done. Negotiating past this point generates diminishing returns.

SHORTCUT

NEGOTIATING DEALS

- **DEFINE** what's on the table in the deal.
- **DECIDE** what's important to you and what's not.
- **HAVE** reasons why those things are important to you.
- **ALWAYS** have a plan B so your hand isn't forced.
- **IF** possible, let the other person open the negotiation.
- **WORK** together rather than digging your heels in.
- **CREATE** a deal that reflects what you both value.
- **STOP** negotiating when the bulk of the deal is defined.

35

How to Handle
Alarming E-mails

Like all communications media, e-mail is imperfect. Like most written media it's ill suited to convey emotion accurately, unless the writer is extremely talented. In addition, e-mail's immediacy makes ill-considered messages inevitable.

This secret explains how to handle three common types of e-mail message that are disturbing to receive and that, if you handle them poorly, can damage your relationships or your career:

1. THE OMINOUS CALL REQUEST

This is when you get a very short message from somebody in authority (such as your boss or a big customer) suggesting that something is wrong and requires your attention, but without providing any details. Examples:

- "We need to talk."
- "Please call me."
- "Big problem."

Since the e-mail is from somebody important, your first reaction is probably to pick up the phone. This is a mistake, for two reasons.

First, while you may be able to guess what's going on, you don't know for certain, so there's a good chance you'll be blindsided. Worst case, you may enter the conversation by addressing a problem that doesn't exist, or didn't until you brought it up.

Second, even if your guess is correct, you don't know enough about how the other person sees the situation to have a productive conversation.

Your best strategy is therefore to provide some times in the near future when conversation can take place, and ask the other person for some details so you can adequately prepare. For example, suppose you get this:

Example:

> **From:** Big Boss
> **Subject:** Conversation
> We need to talk.

WRONG RESPONSE:

> **Subject:** re: Conversation
> BB: Calling you now.

RIGHT RESPONSE:

> **Subject:** re: Conversation
> BB: I'll be free to talk in about 30 minutes.
> Could you give me an idea of what we'll be discuss-
> ing, so I can make certain the conversation is
> productive?

This approach has two advantages. First, you might be able to handle the problem via e-mail, which allows you more time to think about your responses. Second, if you do end up having the conversation, you'll be less likely to make things worse.

2. THE PROVOCATIVE ARGUMENT

Sometimes e-mails are full of "facts" and "observations" that are contrary to your current understanding, consist of out-and-out errors, or contain skewed versions of events or conversations.

For example, suppose you get an e-mail from a coworker accusing you of mishandling a situation that you're pretty certain you handled well.

Your first reaction will probably be a desire to shoot back a withering e-mail providing your side of the argument, and expressing your anger and irritation at having been accused of something untrue and stupid.

However, the result of acting in such a defensive manner is that you can find yourself embroiled in a he-said/she-said e-mail war. Worst case, other people get copied on the e-mail stream, which brings them into the argument.

Rather than taking umbrage and thereby creating more conflict, it's wiser to express that you're confused, need clarification of the facts, and are willing to work on the problem. For example, suppose you receive the following e-mail:

Example:

Subject: Missing Information
You were supposed to provide a requirements document to my department by the end of last week and I haven't seen anything yet. As a result, my engineering group can't make its deadlines.

WRONG RESPONSE:

Subject: re: Missing Information
cc: [Big Boss]

The engineering group's deadlines aren't my concern. If you needed the requirements document by last week, you should have said something two weeks ago. I'm frankly a bit tired of you blaming me for these communications breakdowns.

RIGHT RESPONSE:

Subject: re: Missing Information

I'm confused about this situation because I was not aware that you needed the requirements documents in that time frame. It will take several days to get the requirements together; what's the best way to get engineers back on track?

3. THE FLAME-O-GRAM

These are e-mails chock-full of raw, uncensored negative emotions. They're the electronic equivalent of somebody screaming at you. (See "Secret 7. How to Cope with a Bully.")

After reading this type of e-mail, it's hard not to feel angry in return, or hurt that somebody would be so unkind, or even secretly pleased, because now you have documentation that the other person is a jackass.

However, your best response to flame-o-grams is a combination of empathy and professionalism.

Empathy is appropriate because, in almost every case, whoever sent the e-mail probably regretted it about two seconds after hitting "send." On the other hand, you can't ignore the tone of the e-mail or you're telling the sender that it's OK to vent at you. And that's where your professionalism comes in.

Your challenge is to read through the emotion and find the real problem, so you can address it. At the same time, you must set boundaries so the flamer knows further flames will not be tolerated. For example, suppose you receive the following e-mail:

Example:

Subject: Huge Problem
I can't believe that you guys !$%#! things up so badly again. I just spent an hour on the phone with IBM—our biggest customer—trying to undo the damage that you idiots did to the contract!

WRONG RESPONSE:

Subject: re: Huge Problem
I'm really sorry and am doing everything I can to make it better.

RIGHT RESPONSE:

Subject: re: Huge Problem
I understand that you're upset and I am addressing the problem. That being said, the tone of your e-mail and some of the language you used were unprofessional. I'm sure you'll understand if I ignore any future e-mails that are similarly worded.

Important: wait at least three hours before sending the response. You want to give the hothead some time to cool down (and start feeling stupid) before you draw the boundaries.

ALARMING E-MAILS

- **ASK** for clarification of cryptic conversation requests.
- **PLEAD** confusion to avoid head-to-head confrontation.
- **IF** flamed, address the problem but set boundaries.

PART VI

How to Handle Emergencies

Sometimes "business as usual" isn't. Sooner or later you find yourself in a situation where the normal rules don't apply or where you need quick assistance to fix a problem.

Your ability to deal with such emergencies often depends on how well you've prepared yourself. For example, many emergencies lose their urgency if you've laid the groundwork to quickly find another job (see "Secret 22. How to Achieve Career Security").

That being said, sometimes you need a quick action plan to overcome problems or set your career back on track. This part of the book covers the seven most crucial ones:

■ *"What to Do If You Hate Your Job"* provides a step-by-step process that lets you make certain your negative emotions don't get in the way of either enjoying what you can about your current job or finding a job that suits you better.

■ *"What to Do If You've Screwed Up"* explains how to keep your wits about you when you've made a public mistake, how to keep yourself from making the situation worse, and finally how to apologize effectively and move on.

■ *"What to Do in a Personal Crisis"* is a plan for coping with disasters and problems that suddenly pop up in your personal life. It helps free up the time you'll need to cope, without creating additional problems at work.

■ *"What to Do If There's a Layoff"* helps you identify when a layoff is coming and how you should maneuver and position yourself so it's least likely to affect you, while you simultaneously seek a better job elsewhere.

■ *"What to Do If You're Stressed Out"* explains why you can't afford to have constant stress in your life, followed by a recipe for removing most, if not all, of the stress from your work environment.

■ *"What to Do If You're Fearful"* provides a step-by-step method for moving forward with your plans and goals, even when you're afraid that you might not succeed at the highest level.

■ *"What to Do If You Feel Rejected"* is first aid for the debilitating worry that other people might not like or respect you. You'll learn not just how to ignore rejection, but how to use it to your advantage.

36

What to Do If You Hate Your Job

Many people hate their jobs. However, while it is *common* for people to hate their jobs, it is not *normal*. This is an important distinction. If you believe that it's normal to hate your job, then you'll believe people who don't hate their jobs are *abnormal*.

In reality, some people love their jobs passionately, some hate their jobs passionately, but the majority are shades of indifferent. The process below gets you to this point of indifference (at least), thereby laying the groundwork for finding a job that better suits you:

1. UNDERSTAND THE CORE PROBLEM.

You're probably certain you've got great reasons for hating your job: your boss, your coworkers, your customers, your staff, the repetitiveness, the unpredictability, the long hours, the low pay, whatever.

Those things may be very real challenges, but before you can change them, you've got to get at the core problem, which is the fact that you've let your feelings about your work degenerate into hate, or something that resembles it.

Some people believe that hating a job can be the motivation to get a new one. Maybe so, but there are two problems with this theory:

First, hatred is debilitating rather than motivating. Hating consumes mental and emotional energy that could be better spent finding a job that suits you better. That's why so many people who hate their jobs never seem to do anything about it.

Second, hating your current job makes it more likely that, if you leave, you'll end up in a job that you hate just as much, because when you leave, you'll be taking your emotions with you. As you interview for another job, your hate (and consequent desperation) will cling to you, and your potential future employer will probably sense that something is off.

For example, I have a friend who over a decade had a series of jobs that he hated because (as he put it) "everyone I work for turns out to be a jerk." However, since those jobs were in different industries, what all the jobs had in common was...him.

His anger at his bosses became a self-fulfilling prophesy. When interviewing, he was unable to hide the fact that he blamed his former bosses for his failures. As a result, the only people who'd hire him were lousy bosses who were accustomed to being hated.

The core problem, then, is not your job or your boss or your coworkers, but your emotional reaction to them. You may very well be working in a crummy job, but that's an even better reason to get your emotions under control so you can more easily find something better.

2. CHANGE YOUR MENTAL VOCABULARY.

Many people believe that they experience emotions and then, in order to describe those emotions, select the words that seem the most descriptive. That's true as far as it goes, but there's more to the equation.

Because your mind associates certain words with certain emotions, your words have power to create those emotions as well as describe them. The word *hate* is particularly intense, so the more frequently you think, "I hate my job," the more hatred you create.

Therefore, your first step in getting out of the state of hatred is to select other, less intense words to describe your experience. Here are a few to choose from:

- "I'm uncomfortable in this job."
- "I'm not well suited for this job."
- "I find some parts of my job annoying."

Whenever you hear yourself saying (either to yourself or others) that you "hate" your job, force yourself to substitute the weaker, less intense words. Similarly, suppose you "hate your boss." Rather than fill yourself up with a toxic emotion, weaken it by using phrases that create a more neutral reaction, like these:

- "My boss isn't good with people."
- "My boss has a skewed set of priorities."
- "My boss and I sometimes don't see eye to eye."

De-intensifying the vocabulary that you use to describe your situation doesn't change your situation, of course, but it does keep you from making the experience even worse by over-dramatizing it.

3. FOCUS ON WHAT YOU LIKE ABOUT YOUR JOB.

There's no question that some jobs are truly horrible. However, unless you're in a truly exceptional situation, there are *some* parts of your job that you can manage to like and enjoy. Fortunately, now that you've stopped hypnotizing yourself with hatred, you'll be free to notice them.

List them out, regardless of how small they seem. See how many you can come up with. Make a game out of it, a challenge. Even seemingly trivial stuff is worth listing. Here are some ideas to get you started:

- The first cup of coffee.
- The smile I get from the receptionist each day.
- Knowing that I helped a customer.
- Listening to audiobooks during the commute.
- Realizing I've done my best in a difficult situation.
- Paid vacations and sick days.
- The second cup of coffee.
- Knowing I'm paying my dues.
- Knowing this is temporary and therefore bearable.
- Being amazed and amused at how silly people can be.
- Learning something new about business every day.
- The pleasure of shrugging off nonsense that used to drive me nuts.
- My first cup of decaf.

When you've completed your list, stick a copy of it on your bathroom mirror. Read your list aloud right when you get up and just before you go to bed. Doing so will improve your performance in your current job, making you more valuable both to your current employer and to any future employer. Focusing on the positive will also help provide extra energy that will prove useful in the final step.

4. FIND A JOB THAT BETTER SUITS YOU.

If there's a mismatch between what you need and want, and what your current job is providing to you, you owe it to yourself (not to mention your boss and your current coworkers) to find a different job.

Elsewhere in this book, you'll find "Secret 24. How to Find Your Dream Job" and "Secret 25. How to Land a Job Interview." You'll find those techniques far easier to execute when you're coming from a place of dissatisfaction and amusement rather than hatred and desperation.

IF YOU HATE YOUR JOB

- **YOUR** hate is probably keeping you in the job you hate.
- **REDUCE** your hate by de-intensifying the words you use.
- **FREQUENTLY** repeat everything you like about your job.
- **USE** your better attitude to help you find a better job.

37

What to Do If You've Screwed Up

In the heat of the moment, we blurt out something we wish we hadn't or send an e-mail laced with profanity. Under pressure to perform, we provide half-baked information that leads to bad decisions. Or some other screwup.

Screwing up is part of life. Even great geniuses make mistakes. When you do screw up, however, what's important isn't the screwup (that's history), but what you do afterward. Here's a step-by-step approach:

1. TAKE A DEEP BREATH.

The moment you realize you've made a big mistake is usually *not* the best time to take action to correct it. Any action you take when you're in panic mode is likely to make the problem worse.

For example, suppose you blurt out in a meeting with your boss and Customer A that your company gave Customer B a huge discount. You immediately realize that bringing up that discount means Customer A will probably demand a similar discount.

Trying to recover on the spot is a bad idea. If you tell the customer, "Of course, big discounts aren't our usual policy," you'll only call more attention to the discount. Same thing if you apologize to your boss the moment the two of you leave the meeting.

When you realize you've blundered, your first priority is to get yourself into a resourceful state of mind so you can take the *right* action rather than the *first* action that comes to mind.

So if at all possible take a deep breath, shake yourself out, maybe go for a short walk. Get a little distance from the situation before you react.

In the example above, delaying your reaction gives the situation some time to play out. Perhaps Customer A is less concerned with discounts than with quick delivery, for instance, and thus never brings the matter up.

But suppose Customer A *does* demand a discount. In this case you might point out to your boss that big discounts have a tendency to become public knowledge anyway and that by bringing it up, you were preventing a future problem in the relationship with Customer A.

You're much more likely to come up with a "creative solution" to your gaffe when you're not caught up in your own embarrassment at making it.

2. TAKE A DOSE OF PERSPECTIVE.

If you're like most people, your imagination is probably conjuring up a worst-case scenario. However, while your blunder may seem monumental to you, it may be far less significant to the other people involved.

If your mistake is uncharacteristic of you, chances are that people who already know you will simply put it down to your having a bad day. That doesn't mean you don't need to make amends, but the situation may be less dire than you assume.

Furthermore, ten years from now—heck, probably ten days from now—people will have probably forgotten all about your mistake.

For example, I once had a conversation with a boss of mine in which I later felt I'd been completely unreasonable, putting pressure on him and making him look bad right when he was struggling to keep his own job, which he soon lost.

I felt *terrible* about that conversation for a decade before I got up the nerve to call the guy and apologize. Turns out he didn't even remember it. While it loomed enormous in my mind, he'd long since moved on.

Understanding that your huge, embarrassing mistake is insignificant in the grand scheme of things helps you put your subsequent fix-it attempts into perspective. Yes, you want to make amends, but there's no reason to go overboard.

3. DO A REALITY CHECK.

Now that you've gotten some distance and perspective, revisit your blunder with one or more of the other people who witnessed it. Because you want to find out how much damage has been done, put your inquiry in the form of a question. Examples:

■ "John, when I reacted negatively to your idea earlier today, I think I might have been overly harsh. I want to make certain you know that I'm not trying to be a pill and that my heart is in the right place."

■ "Joe, I just discovered that there was some inaccurate data in yesterday's presentation. Am I correct in assuming that there's time for me to provide new data before a final decision is made?"

■ "James, I'm concerned that the joke I told during our last staff meeting might have seemed inappropriate to some of the attendees. What's your reading of the situation?"

Reality checks are best delivered via e-mail rather than in person, because e-mail provides distance from the emotions of the moment, giving both you and the other person the opportunity to assess the actual importance of the blunder.

4. APOLOGIZE AND ADDRESS THE BLOWBACK.

The response that you get from your reality check in the previous step lets you gauge what you'll need to do in order to get past the mistake. For example, if the response is something like "You screwed up badly, you jerk," you'll need to do some groveling.

On the other hand, if the response is more like "Yeah, I was offended/angry/surprised but it's no big deal," your apology can be more perfunctory. In either case, your apology provides an opening to address whatever actual problem (if any) your blunder created.

Here are some examples:

- "John, I'm really sorry that I overreacted and would like to meet with you to apologize in person and make a commitment to never allow myself to act that way in the future."
- "Joe, I'm sorry for the oversight. I've attached a corrected presentation with the correct data highlighted and have sent this presentation to all attendees. What else can we do to mitigate the damage?"
- "James, I feel like a clueless idiot for making that dumb joke and it won't happen again. What's the best way for everyone to move beyond this?"

As a general rule, groveling works better in person or on the phone rather than in an e-mail. The main thing, though, is to apologize for screwing up and then move on.

WHEN YOU'VE SCREWED UP

■ **DON'T** try to fix things immediately; take some time to think.

■ **REMEMBER** that eventually nobody will care what happened.

■ **FIND** out how seriously you screwed up.

■ **MAKE** apologies but focus on fixing the results.

38

What to Do in a Personal Crisis

A personal crisis is something unexpected that requires extra physical and emotional attention: an illness, a death in the family, a tax audit, etc. Since such events happen to everybody, this secret explains how to prepare ahead of time and what to do when a crisis actually hits.

1. OBSERVE YOUR BOSS'S TOLERANCE.

Every boss has a level of tolerance when it comes the intrusion of a personal crisis into the work routine. Some bosses are understanding of the occasional crisis, while others only care that the work gets done.

To discover your current boss's tolerance level, observe how he or she reacts when other people encounter personal crises. Whatever level of sympathy and empathy you observe from your boss is exactly what you can expect when it's your turn.

For example, I once had a boss who accused me of "goofing off" when I was absent from work for a week in order to recover from nasal surgery. I was surprised and alarmed, but I shouldn't have been, because he'd been similarly unsympathetic to my coworkers.

Knowing how your boss tends to react provides guidance for how much groundwork you need to lay to protect yourself in the event that you experience a crisis.

If you are one of the lucky few who still get paid vacation days, it's prudent to hang on to a few of those days, just in case you need them. Since you're owed them, it's harder for a boss to complain if you suddenly need to take them.

2. HABITUALLY FINISH PROJECTS EARLY.

If you get in the habit of waiting until the last minute to complete your projects, even a minor crisis—like a head cold—can mean that you'll miss your deadline. If you regularly complete your projects early, you've got some "padding" if something goes wrong.

However—and this is important—if you simply *hand in* all your projects early, your boss will move all your subsequent project deadlines forward, thereby eliminating your padding. Instead, get your projects done early, hold on to them until the deadline, then turn them in.

Just to be clear, I am *not* suggesting that you pad your time estimates in order to goof off. Instead, I'm recommending that you use the extra time to work on future projects, thereby making it easier to get those future projects done early too.

A side benefit of finishing up before your deadlines: it gives you time to think about the project a bit before you turn it in. When I do this, I usually think of a few quick changes that make the final result far better than if I'd waited until the last minute.

However, the main reason for habitually finishing projects early is that it allows you to create the ideal crisis management situation, which is one in which you can cope with the crisis without anybody at work really noticing that anything's wrong.

3. KEEP SOME FAVORS TO CALL IN.

In "Secret 9. How to Play Clean Office Politics" I explain how to collect favors and keep track of who owes you what. A reason for having people owe you favors is that you can call them in when you're in a pinch: "Hey, something came up at home that I've got to handle. Could you finish up the Acme project for me?"

That's a reasonable request if you've helped that coworker out, or if you're certain (and your coworker is certain) that you'll be able to return the favor later, as evidenced by the fact that the two of you have traded favors in the past.

Please note that asking for help with your work is *not* the same as asking your coworkers for emotional support. I may sound heartless, but your coworkers don't want to deal with your personal problems. They've got their own problems to worry about.

Sharing details of your personal crisis while at work increases the negative impact of that crisis on your workplace. If your coworker is truly concerned, empathy will make his or her work suffer too. If not, you're just being a bore.

Even worse, your coworkers may see your crisis as an opportunity to advance their own careers, such as getting your plum assignments reassigned to them.

Rather than depending on coworkers for emotional support, I recommend creating and maintaining an entirely separate support network of non-work friends, family, health-care providers, and so forth.

4. RENEGOTIATE YOUR PRIORITIES.

If the groundwork you've laid is insufficient to allow you to handle the personal crisis, you'll need to work with your boss to change your deadlines, reassign projects, and generally ensure that your crisis doesn't intrude on everyone else.

The best way to approach the negotiation is to make it about getting the work done, not making your life easier. If possible, come into the discussion with a solution rather than just an announcement that your personal life has created a problem.

Of course, this is difficult to do when you're simultaneously dealing with a personal crisis. The last thing you need, frankly, is to be worrying about work priorities that probably seem trivial in comparison. To you, anyway.

But probably not to your boss and your coworkers. While they may feel some sympathy and empathy, they still have to get their own jobs done, meet their own deadlines, and now (probably) take on your work as well.

Therefore, you should try to make at least a good-faith effort to figure out how you can cope with your crisis without inconveniencing everyone else. That being said, there's a point at which you gotta do what you gotta do.

Deal with your crisis, even if it means blowing off work, missing your deadlines, and forcing everyone else at work to adapt. As long as you've tried to limit the impact of your problem, you can cope with it with a clean conscience.

Take care of yourself. They'll manage without you.

SHORTCUT

HANDLING A PERSONAL CRISIS

- **GET** a feeling for how much empathy you'll get.
- **MAKE** a habit of finishing your projects early.
- **DO** favors for others that you can call in when necessary.
- **IF** a crisis hits, try to minimize the damage at work.
- **DO** what you must to take care of yourself.

39

What to Do If There's a Layoff

Contrary to popular belief, a layoff in your company need not be a personal disaster. In fact, if you prepare ahead of time and keep your wits, you use the situation to your advantage. Here's how.

1. HEED THE WARNING SIGNS.

When layoffs happen, many people are unprepared because they'd rather not face the truth. Emotionally, it's much easier to accept the assurances of management that everything is proceeding according to plan and your job is not in jeopardy.

However, you always want to make career decisions based on reality, and the reality is that layoffs are usually preceded by any or all of the following:

- *Several quarters of financial loss.* When an established company has a single unprofitable quarter, it's no big deal. A series of such quarters, however, means that whatever actions management is taking to fix the problem aren't working, which means it will probably resort to layoffs to reduce expenses.
- *Management visits to third world countries.* Unless there's a compelling reason (like the presence of a big customer) for management

to be flying to parts of the world where labor is cheap, it's highly likely that your company is in the planning phase of a major outsourcing. Layoffs are inevitable as the jobs migrate.

■ *A merger or acquisition.* Companies merge with or acquire other firms with the intent that the whole (after the merger) will make more money than the sum of the parts. This usually involves "eliminating redundancies" (i.e., layoffs). Since many mergers and acquisitions eventually fail, the result is often even more layoffs.

■ *Private equity investment.* The private equity business model consists of (1) purchasing a company using the company's assets as collateral, (2) increasing the company's value through layoffs, and (3) selling off the company (or its parts) at a profit, which usually results in even more layoffs.

■ *Official denials of layoff rumors.* Unlike other corporate rumors, a layoff rumor doesn't create much of an advantage for anybody, which is why they're usually true. Top management denies such rumors only when it's taking them seriously, which again happens only if the rumors reflect reality.

2. DEVELOP ALTERNATIVES ELSEWHERE.

If any of the above red flags pop up, activate your escape plan immediately. (See "Secret 22. How to Achieve Career Security.") If you wait you'll end up competing with all your coworkers for the same jobs, because they've probably got most of the same contacts that you've got.

Similarly, if you've been thinking about starting your own company, this is the time to get serious. Write your business plan, seek out investors, and get everything lined up so you're ready to jump, if it's necessary to do so.

3. MAKE YOURSELF INDISPENSABLE.

While you're developing other opportunities, find ways to make yourself even more valuable to your management.

One easy way to do this is to remain calm during the crisis. Since there will be plenty of weird emotions floating around before and during the layoffs, anybody who keeps contributing (rather than freezing up in fright) is likely to be valued.

Beyond that, increase your contribution, especially in areas that your boss finds personally difficult. For example, if your boss lacks the technical chops to command the respect of the engineers, become your boss's spokesperson to that group.

Yes, it's challenging to do this while you're simultaneously developing other opportunities. Unfortunately, this is one of those situations in which you may have to sacrifice your personal life, at least for a while.

4. CONSIDER A LATERAL MOVE.

If you can't become indispensable, consider moving into a group that's less likely to bear the brunt of a layoff. If the layoff is due to a merger or outsourcing, you should move into whatever group is least likely to be affected.

For example, suppose you work in customer service and your top management has been having meetings with a firm in Pakistan that specializes in customer service. This is a good time to make the move into sales or marketing.

Similarly, suppose you're working in the marketing group and your company has just acquired a firm that manufactures a product intended to be sold alongside your current product set. There will undoubtedly be redundancies in marketing, so consider moving into engineering.

Having observed layoffs in several large companies, I have noticed that they tend to take place in the following order:

1. *Clerical support.* While the people who work directly with the top managers will survive (if their managers do), the rest of the staff is decimated.

2. *Marketing.* The marketers go first because they're usually seen as providing a service to the sales group rather than performing a strategic function.

3. *Customer support.* The support team goes next because management can always pretend that customers will be forgiving until the company gets back on its feet.

4. *Manufacturing.* Since your company isn't making money, you've probably been stockpiling product that hasn't been sold. Why manufacture more?

5. *Engineering.* Since the engineers represent the future of your company, they go when your management concludes the future won't happen.

6. *Sales.* At this point things have become so desperate that your company is firing the people who make the money, in order to save money.

7. *Human resources.* Hey, somebody has to handle all the paperwork and legal issues as your company proceeds to destroy itself.

That being said, very stupid companies run by very stupid executives tend to do very stupid things, such as firing the sales force before firing the marketing folk.

5. TAKE THE PACKAGE (IF OFFERED).

Making yourself indispensable and moving to a relatively safe group are defensive moves intended to keep you employed until you can find something better elsewhere.

Make no mistake about it: layoffs are the death knell, if not for your company then probably for any chance of enjoying work or experiencing career growth.

Most of the time, layoffs create a downward spiral, ending only in bankruptcy or some other company's acquiring the shell of what your company originally was.

Even if that doesn't happen, things are going to be unpleasant at best. Your company will ask for longer hours, give lower salary increases (or even decrease your pay), and eliminate whatever small perks you might be enjoying.

Furthermore, the longer you remain, the more failure starts to cling to you. Best you get out while the rest of the world thinks your company might be the comeback kid, instead of waiting until it's roadkill.

While the practice seems to have become less common, some companies still begin the layoff process by asking for volunteers, and giving them incentives to leave.

If you're offered a package, take it. Chances are that if you remain, you'll still get laid off but without the extra benefits.

I worked with a guy who was offered a severance package of two weeks' pay for each of the twenty-five years he'd worked for the company—basically an entire year's salary.

He passed on the package, hoping to keep his current job, without bothering to line up anything else. Two (miserable) years later he was canned with minimal severance.

6. LAND A POSITION ELSEWHERE.

The perfect scenario is for you to take the severance package and go to work someplace better the next day. The next-best scenario is for you to hang on to your job until you find something better. The worst-case scenario is for you to get laid off without having lined anything else up.

Regardless of which scenario plays itself out, there's a unifying element: you're outta there. But let's suppose that it's the worst-case scenario. As a very wise man once told me: "Everyone I've ever known who got laid off was upset when it happened but within eighteen months was saying it was the best thing that ever happened to them."

COPING WITH LAYOFFS

- **KNOW** when a layoff is coming and plan accordingly.
- **MAKE** certain you've got some other options.
- **WHEN** it happens, don't panic. Make yourself useful.
- **IF** possible, move into a group that's unlikely to bear the brunt.
- **IF** you're offered a voluntary severance package, take it.
- **ACCEPT** a job elsewhere as soon as you find a good one.

40

What to Do If You're Stressed Out

Stress can result in headaches, muscle tension, muscle pain, chest pain, fatigue, upset stomach, insomnia, anxiety, restlessness, lack of motivation, lack of focus, irritability, depression, eating problems, addiction, and social withdrawal—here's how to avoid it:

1. WORK FORTY HOURS A WEEK (OR FEWER).

Many companies and industries have cultures that encourage salaried employees to regularly work unpaid overtime (i.e., more than forty hours a week). Unfortunately, if you let that culture determine your behavior, you'll end up wasting time and adding stress.

It's a myth that you can consistently get more done by working longer hours. In the early 1900s, Ford Motor ran dozens of tests on workers and discovered that working sixty hours a week (rather than forty) provides only a short-term increase in productivity. After three to four weeks of working the long hours, people working sixty hours a week end up getting *less* done than when they were working forty hours a week, because they become stressed out and start making avoidable errors.

Workaholics may think they're accomplishing more than the less fanatical, but in fact, long hours result in stressed-out people who get too sick to work, and who produce sloppy work that must be either scrapped or redone.

2. AVOID STRESSED-OUT PEOPLE.

Your brain is programmed to reflect the behaviors of those you see and hear. This is a neurological phenomenon resulting from the *mirror neurons* in your brain. In other words, you can "catch" stress from other people.

So although it may not be possible to avoid stressed people all the time, you should try, as far as possible, to limit your contact with such people—at least until you've conquered your own stress.

At that point the opposite effect kicks in, because the calmness you will have achieved is also contagious—provided you've made it into a strong enough habit. In other words, reducing your own stress can help everyone around you do the same.

3. CREATE AND VISIT AN OASIS.

In the past, people worked nine to five; in today's business environments, there's pressure to work (or at least be available) 24-7. Needless to say, that pressure generates oodles of stress.

An absurdly easy way to reduce that stress is to shut down your computer and your cell—not just while you sleep, but also an hour before and after you sleep. This takes discipline, because you're probably in the habit of checking e-mail, texts, and so forth all the time.

Doing this also takes self-confidence, because you must believe that you don't need to be at the constant beck and call of your boss, colleagues, and customers.

4. DISCONNECT FROM THE UNCONTROLLABLE.

If you're like most people, a huge amount of your stress comes from worrying about events that you simply can't control: the economy, the weather, traffic, politics, other people's thoughts and emotions, customer decisions, and so forth.

While it can be useful to observe and predict such events (in order to know how to react to them), once you've decided how you'll deal with them, it's stressful (and, frankly, a little nuts) to obsess about them.

Worrying about stuff you can't control isn't going to make any difference either in the short or the long run. It's wasted energy and extra stress you don't need. Change what you can change and shrug off what you can't.

5. RENEGOTIATE YOUR WORKLOAD.

Unreasonable expectations about what you're capable of accomplishing are a huge source of stress—regardless of whether those expectations come from yourself, your boss, or your customers.

The cure for this kind of stress is a dose of reality. Look at how much time you've got to spend, assess the amount of work that needs to be done, and, based on that, be realistic about what's actually going to get done.

If you're expected to accomplish A, B, C, and D, and there's only time to achieve three of the four, decide—or force your boss to decide—which three will actually get done and which one will not.

6. TURN OFF THE NEWS.

The news, like every other form of entertainment, makes money by producing strong emotions in its audience. Outside of business news, those emotions are almost exclusively negative: anger, fear, anxiety, dread, and frustration.

While those manufactured emotions do provide momentary distraction from work stress, they do it by adding more stress. Watching or listening to the news in order "to relax" is like having a beer to dull the pain of a hangover.

So whenever you come upon a news story that starts to make you angry or upset, change the channel—unless it's 100 percent relevant to your life—or click to another page.

7. LEARN TO SAY NO.

Many people feel stressed because they "have way too much work to do." That sounds perfectly reasonable, but in fact it's not the work that's creating the stress. It's worrying about what might happen if all that work doesn't get done.

I once heard that when you commit to 10 percent more than you can actually accomplish, it feels as if you've got 50 percent more, thereby creating *even more stress*. I don't know whether that's true, but I have observed that taking on too much work makes me feel as if things might fall apart if I (gasp!) take a day off.

It's not enough to be able to say no to your boss and your coworkers. Sometimes the real challenge is learning to say no to yourself when you're tempted to over-commit. Like any good habit, this becomes easier over time.

8. REMAIN IN THE HERE AND NOW.

Probably the biggest source of stress is worrying about the future. While it's a good idea to have a plan, you'll be better able to execute that plan if you don't think all that much about that future.

Being focused on the present eliminates stress even when disaster strikes. Suppose, in the middle of your workday, you get news that your biggest customer is jumping ship. You could react to the news by freaking out, of course.

Or you could remain in the moment, note that the event happened, continue with whatever you're doing—and then, when you're relaxed and feeling creative, devise a step-by-step plan to win the customer back or find some new customers.

9. NEVER ARGUE WITH FOOLS OR STRANGERS.

When you're driving, you're going to see people driving in ways that are stupid, dangerous, and annoying. Even so, you're wasting your energy getting upset about what they do, to say nothing of reacting to it by honking or flipping the bird.

Similarly, getting into arguments with people online (such as in the comments sections of blogs or underneath controversial articles) is a colossally foolish way to spend your time. Do you really care what some stranger thinks?

I'd venture to say that in the entire history of the Internet there has not been a single time when anybody online has changed the opinion of anybody else. Online squabbling is always a waste of time.

10. AVOID MULTITASKING.

Trying to do multiple things at once gives you the illusion that you're getting a lot of things done, when in fact those things are getting done badly. The result is stress, not just because you're trying to do too much at once, but because you know (in your heart) that the work you're doing isn't (and can't be) your best.

By contrast, focusing on one thing, getting it done, and doing it well gives you a sense of accomplishment and mental serenity. It puts *you*, rather than the demands of everything else around you, in control of your life.

REDUCING STRESS

- **WORKING** more than forty hours a week quickly becomes unproductive.
- **STRESS** is contagious so avoid people who won't control theirs.
- **FIND** a place where you can get away from work activity.
- **DEVELOP** the patience and perspective to let go of your results.
- **IF** you're overworked, make your workload more reasonable.
- **OTHER** than business news, news saps your energy.
- **AVOID** projects that you can't do well.
- **FOCUS** on what you're doing now rather than the results.
- **ARGUING** with fools and strangers is completely useless.
- **MULTITASKING** is tiresome and prevents you from doing any task well.

What to Do If You're Fearful

Most people aren't as successful as they might be, simply because their fear is keeping them from taking action.

Fear of rejection, fear of failure, fear of mistakes, fear of the boss's temper, fear, fear, fear... it doesn't matter what scares you: if you're afraid, you don't take the risks necessary to make you successful.

Fear is normal and useful. It's a signal that you need to be careful and think things through. More important, it can create the energy and excitement you need to push yourself to the next level. Here's how it's done:

1. INCREASE YOUR FAMILIARITY.

The more you do confront and deal with something that scares you, the less frightening it becomes. For example, psychologists who treat debilitating phobias (such as claustrophobia) expose their patients to what's frightening them, gradually and with increasing frequency.

The same principle applies in the workplace when you *must* do something that frightens you. For instance, many beginning salespeople who must cold-call to develop opportunities begin with a fear that they'll be rejected.

Over time, however, the salespeople who become good at cold

calling overcome that fear because they've experienced the rejection and realize that it's no big deal.

Another common workplace situation is a fear of saying no when asked to take on projects, even when those projects are unreasonable. As I explained in "Secret 6. How to Handle Unreasonable Requests," saying no gets easier the more you do it.

The wonderful thing about increasing your familiarity with a fear is that it's automatic. As long as you don't allow fear to paralyze you, you end up dealing with it one way or another, thereby making it less daunting.

2. REHEARSE COURAGE MENTALLY.

It's a physiological fact that your brain can't differentiate between emotions that emerge from your imagination and emotions that are produced by events in the outside world. *Emotions are what you're doing, not what's being done to you.*

Therefore, if you repeatedly imagine something that you fear, while at the same time visualizing yourself as calm, confident, and collected while dealing with that fear, you're training your mind to act the same way when real-world events take place.

For example, suppose you're afraid of speaking in public. If you vividly imagine yourself giving a speech that's articulate and interesting, feeling the emotion that comes from the imagined applause, that confidence will reappear when you're actually at the lectern.

3. REFRAME YOUR FEAR.

The frame of a picture creates a boundary that puts the picture into context and tells you what's important in it. For example, a frame that cuts out all but one person in a group photo changes it from a group photo into a portrait.

The same thing is true with emotions—the "frame" you build around them determines how you experience those emotions.

For example, imagine being trapped, helpless, in a tiny metal box, with only your head, shoulders, and arms sticking out, falling over a cliff. Imagine the feeling of falling faster and faster, and the hard, cold ground coming up at you, faster and faster. Pretty scary, eh?

It's called a roller coaster. The "reframe" involves understanding that you got on the ride of your own free will, you almost undoubtedly aren't going to hit the ground, and, most important, you're having fun!

Or take the common fear of public speaking. Most performing artists feel similar "butterflies" before a performance, but they turn their nervousness into energy just before going onstage. After all, you're nervous only if you care about your results.

4. MAKE THE FEAR USEFUL.

Finally, far from being debilitating, fear is an enabling emotion. As I mentioned previously, fear is a signal that you must take action. It may sound trite, but there's real truth to the old saying: "Feel the fear, then do it anyway."

This applies to a vast range of business situations. For example, if a salesperson is afraid to ask for the business, it is a sign that the conversation is getting to the point at which it will be necessary to ask. That's useful information.

Similarly, if you feel afraid of losing an oxymoronic "secure job," it's a sign that the job to which you're clinging is no longer serving your needs.

I went through that myself when I left the corporate world to become a professional writer. I was terrified but I knew what I wanted. I laid the groundwork and then did what I had to do—quit. If I hadn't, you wouldn't be reading this book!

HARNESSING FEAR

- **THE** more frequently you confront a fear, the less power it has.
- **IMAGINE** dealing with the fear to make it less daunting.
- **REMEMBER** that fear is just excitement in disguise.
- **USE** the fear to give you energy to perform.

SECRET **42**

What to Do If You Feel
Rejected

Every significant business endeavor involves other people, and that
means a risk of rejection, because when you put yourself out there,
you're setting yourself up to get turned down.

Because of this, the fear of rejection prevents many people from
taking action that could greatly improve their circumstances. This
chapter explains not just how to take the sting out of rejection, but
how to use it as a means to your larger goals.

1. REALIZE THAT REJECTION IS AN ILLUSION.

Rejection is an emotionally loaded term that people unwisely use
when they fail to achieve a goal that involves another person. Nobody
feels "rejected" when they set a goal to, say, run a four-minute mile,
but then end up running it in five minutes.

The concept of rejection implies that there's something personal
about the failure, but that's just an illusion. What's actually happened is that a goal wasn't achieved because the two people involved
had different rules about life. This is an impersonal fact.

For example, suppose you make a cold call and the other person
swears at you and hangs up. Suppose the call starts out good but you

say something the other person thinks is stupid and he or she hangs up on you.

While those outcomes aren't ideal, they're only "rejection" because you've decided to feel bad about them.

Stuff happens. Often other people are involved. Sometimes you might have done something differently and gotten a different outcome. But in every case, the "rejection" happened because you accidentally violated the other person's rules. In other words, the sense of being rejected is just a weird trick that your emotions are playing on you.

2. EXTRACT THE STING FROM THE REJECTION.

Every time I've pointed out the simple reality in Step 1, somebody has come back with something like, "But I still feel rejected." Usually in a whiny voice.

People *do* feel rejected, and it's always for the same reason: they've invested their time and energy into creating a negative mental picture of what it means if they don't achieve a particular goal with a particular person.

So think about it: why do you feel rejected? What's so important about this event that you're treating it as something that threatens your opinion of yourself and indeed your own identity?

If you step back from the situation, you'll find that the sting of rejection comes from your rules about other people.

- "After about the fifth bad cold call, I'm ready to call it a day."
- "If I'm close enough to ask a customer for a favor, rejection would hurt."
- "C-level job holders are important, so their opinion of me matters."

You feel "rejected" (i.e., bad) because you're treating your rules as if they're incredibly important, while discounting the fact that the other person has rules too, which you can't possibly understand completely.

To remove the sting of rejection, question those beliefs and, ideally, replace them with better beliefs that inspire confidence rather than fear. Examples:

- "Every cold call is a new opportunity; the past is the past."
- "A relationship that's not worth risking isn't worth having."
- "Coping with cranky executives means I'm playing in the big leagues."

3. REFRAME EACH REJECTION AS A STEPPING-STONE.

Sometimes success is just a numbers game. As has been pointed out innumerable times, Reggie Jackson, one of the greatest hitters of all time, also holds the Major League Baseball record for being struck out.

When I wanted to publish my first business book, I sent the proposal to dozens of editors and got plenty of "rejection" letters. Rather than feeling discouraged, I started each day by laying out the letters on the floor and walking on them as if they were stepping-stones.

As I did this, I'd say to myself, "The more rejections I get, the better the deal I'll get." Sure enough, the book got picked up by Random House, and its eventual publication launched my professional writing career.

My mother, who had a very successful career in sales, stuck Post-its in her car and on her bathroom mirror with slogans like "REJECTION = MONEY." She had realized that there is no easy path to long-term success.

Looking at rejection as part of success forces you to focus away from the "rejection" and on the issues that are under your control.

For example, if you're not getting the investors you need, review your business plan with an expert or find a better role model to imitate. If your cold calls are consistently falling flat, work on your script. Rather than feeling rejected, try different approaches.

SHORTCUT

TRANSCENDING REJECTION

■ **REJECTION** only means the other person had different rules.

■ **REJECTION** stings because you've made the other person too important.

■ **EVERY** rejection inevitably moves you closer to your goal.

VII

How to Cope
with Evil

As much as we all wish it weren't so, there's plenty of evil floating around in the business world. This final part is your guide to identifying that evil and protecting yourself from its worst effects.

Please note that the information in this part is dangerous, because it's impossible to identify some kinds of evil without explaining how to do evil things. For example, when I tell you how to spot a dirty political trick, I'm also telling you how to play that trick.

I strongly advise that you not use these secrets to do evil yourself. Remember: you're going to have to live with yourself, and if you act like an asshole, you end up living with an asshole...you. With that warning in mind, here's what you'll learn:

■ *"How to Thwart Dirty Office Politics"* protects you from bosses, coworkers, and employees who attempt to manipulate you into doing what they want when it's not in your best interest.

■ *"How to Cope with Management Fads"* reveals the truth about management consultants and the expensive methods they recommend, as well as how to either avoid or sidestep these exercises in futility.

■ *"How to Spot a Workplace Lie"* gives you the tools you need to tell when you're being lied to (even when the liar is technically telling the truth), so you can make your own plans without being fooled.

■ *"How to Identify a Bogus Statistic"* lists the most common ways businesspeople manipulate quantitative facts in order to distort the truth, mislead other employees, or distort and even "prove" a falsehood.

■ *"The Eight Lies Most Bosses Tell"* explains the falsehoods that continually crop up in the boss/employee relationship, why those falsehoods exist, and what you should know when they appear in your workplace.

■ *"The Seven Times It's OK to Lie to the Boss"* presents the times when reality trumps morality—specific situations in which you're justified in keeping the truth from your boss and others at your workplace.

■ *"How to Safely Be a Whistle-Blower"* explains what to do when you discover that your company is doing something unethical or illegal—without utterly destroying your career in the process.

How to Thwart Dirty Office Politics

Some people believe that the way to get what they want is to manipulate other people by playing dirty politics. This secret reveals the nine most common of these dirty tricks, as well as your best defenses against them.

1. DEVELOPMENT OPPORTUNITIES

The *development opportunity* is a trick bosses play on an employee when they want that employee to take on a job or project that he or she would normally avoid.

Development opportunities are not real assignments that might allow you to show your value to the boss or the rest of the company. They're donkey work packaged as an educational experience.

There are two types of "development opportunities"—those given to current employees and those given to new workers (specifically interns).

Development opportunities directed at the currently employed are the crap jobs that need doing but that nobody wants to do. Why did the boss pick on you? Chances are you don't push back as much as your coworkers.

There's also a real possibility that the boss is dumping lousy assignments on you in order to get you to quit, which saves the boss the time and trouble of doing the paperwork to get you fired.

Development opportunities directed at new workers take the form of the infamous unpaid internship. Every year tens of thousands of workplace novices are convinced that it's in their interest to work for free, in the naive belief that this will help them get a job.

Sure, there are interns who landed a job after working for free. However, they most likely got those jobs *despite* working for free, not *because* of it. Just ask the thousands of interns who never get offered a paid gig.

The moment you agree to work for free, you're setting the value of your labor to exactly zero. Working for free, or on the cheap, simply reduces the value of your labor to free or cheap.

2. ROCK FETCHES

A *rock fetch* is when a boss asks an employee to create or obtain a useless object or series of useless objects as a precondition to the manager's making a certain decision. The fetching process allows the boss to avoid making that decision.

Rocks have two characteristics: they're hard and they're useless. Whenever a boss asks you to do or get something before he or she makes a decision, step back and assess the difficulty and usefulness of whatever you're being asked to do.

If the request is for something reasonable (such as a go-ahead from another manager whose group might be affected), you're not on a rock fetch. If the request is for something absurd, such as a fifty-page report to get the approval to move to another cubicle, you're on a rock fetch.

Whenever you suspect you're on a rock fetch, ask yourself why your boss might not want to make the decision you want made. Would it change the status quo? Would it weaken the boss's power or limit the boss's options? Try to find the root of the problem.

Figuring out the root is almost always a better use of your time and energy than fetching the rock. When you think you know why the boss would prefer to avoid the decision, confirm the root problem by asking about it. Example: "I sense that you're uncomfortable with this decision. Are there some politics involved that I don't know about?"

By probing for the root of the problem, you can propel the discussion out of the realm of manipulation and into the realm of working with your boss to accomplish a common goal.

3. SACRIFICIAL LAMBS

A boss or a coworker might set you up as a *sacrificial lamb* in order to take the heat if something goes wrong but take the credit if something goes right.

For example, suppose your coworker wants to float a potentially controversial idea at a meeting with your mutual boss but is afraid he'll lose credibility if the CEO thinks the idea stupid. An easy way to test the waters is to get you to present the idea instead.

Your coworker helps you prepare the slides, making certain that the controversial proposal is positioned so it looks as if it's your idea. If the idea gets shot down at the meeting, your coworker joins in and takes some potshots to show solidarity with the boss.

However, if the idea is well received, your coworker inserts himself into the discussion and takes credit for it, perhaps by making a remark like, "Jim, you did a great job presenting my idea; why don't I take over and provide the details?"

Please note this trick works only if you let yourself get maneuvered into "owning" an idea that isn't yours. Therefore, the easiest way to defend against it is to preemptively give credit wherever it's due.

So rather than saying something like, "This chart shows that selling explosives online will increase our revenue by 100 percent," say something like, "This chart shows Fred's estimates of the revenue increase that might result from online sales of our explosives."

If the idea gets shot down, you make it clear (again) that the idea belongs to Fred rather than to you. Same thing if the idea gets kudos. Fair is fair.

This maneuver is more dicey if the person setting you up is your boss, because it's usually a bad idea to throw your boss under the bus. ("'Vengeance is mine,' sayeth the ~~Lord~~ Boss.") Therefore, use this maneuver after you've told your boss that you're happy to be the mouthpiece but not the fall guy.

4. FORCING A CARD

About half the card tricks in the lexicon of stage magic depend on the ability of the performer to ensure that a volunteer picks a particular card, even though it appears to the audience as if the selection is random. This is called *forcing a card*.

The business-world equivalent is when somebody (usually somebody who works for you) prepares three alternative approaches to a problem so it appears to you that there's a choice, when actually only one of the approaches makes any real sense.

For example, suppose an employee wants you to hire his college friend. He recommends three candidates: (1) his friend, (2) an unqualified person who will need lots of training, and (3) an overqualified person who's likely to leave when a better offer comes along. You choose the friend, thinking you made a good decision when in fact the decision was forced.

The challenge here, for your employee, was to make the two lousy choices plausible enough to warrant your serious consideration without making them plausible enough for you to actually select one of the two non-starters.

The challenge for you is to recognize when you're being presented with false alternatives. If this happens, refuse to accept the list. Say something like, "I wanted three real alternatives and what you've given me here is one that's viable and two that aren't."

In all probability the other person will get defensive and claim that the alternatives are real and so forth. Ignore this, then say: "Be honest: are you trying to force my hand? Because I really do want some real choices."

Your goal is to insert honesty into the relationship while letting the other person understand that you don't intend to be manipulated.

5. HIDING SKELETONS

Hiding skeletons is when an employee or coworker possesses information that he or she doesn't want you to know but that you'd have every right to be angry at that person if you learned you hadn't been told.

For example, suppose you're the boss of an engineering group and one of your engineers learns that the product he designed has a higher-than-normal failure rate. However, the engineer is up for promotion, which will be jeopardized if you find out.

In this case the engineer might elect to provide that information to you in such a way that the implications of that information are not immediately clear. The engineer will then get his promotion and, when (or if) the bad news emerges into daylight, the engineer can claim he told you all about it.

Skeleton-hiding is generally accomplished through locating the toxic information near the end (but not *at* the end) of a long e-mail or report. Another method consists of burying the toxic information in plain sight through the use of technical jargon and biz-blab.

Finding hidden skeletons is mostly a matter of common sense combined with careful observation. When you receive a long report that might contain something problematic, click to the end of the document, then click back a few paragraphs. If there's a skeleton, that's usually where you'll find it.

A red flag should also go up in your brain whenever somebody who usually communicates clearly suddenly lapses into semicomprehensible jargon. When confronted with such jargon, your best approach is to ask, point-blank: "What does this mean in plain language?"

For example, suppose you run across something like this near the end of a long e-mail:

> "An analysis of field-gathered anecdotal evidence
> indicates that our manufacturables, either through
> improper usage, a combination of proper and
> improper usage, or even recommended usage, could
> and may result in consequential events and even,
> under limited circumstances, the unintentional
> vital discontinuity of those using, having used, or
> attempting to use them."

You could just skim the paragraph and forget it, which is exactly what the skeleton-hider is hoping you'll do. Rather than doing this, though, press the person who wrote the gibberish to clarify what the paragraph really means. (In this case, the skeleton being hidden is "Our product is killing customers.")

6. RATHOLING A MEETING

When somebody doesn't like where a meeting is headed, he or she may try to change the subject by bringing up an issue that's guaranteed to distract everyone. This is known as *ratholing a meeting*.

For example, suppose your meeting is to review a project's status, but Jill hasn't gotten much done. Rather than take the heat, Jill brings up a rumor that your firm's biggest customer may leave for another vendor.

Suddenly the project review meeting turns into a planning session to avoid the impending disaster. That discussion consumes the remainder of the meeting, leaving the late project still to be reviewed at some future date (when Jill will presumably be more prepared).

Ratholes work only when whoever is running the meeting is willing to jump down them. If you have an agenda for every meeting and stick to that agenda, your meetings will stay on course, even when people bring up distracting issues.

Whenever you sense a rathole opening, state that you realize the rathole is an important issue (even if it's not) and then table it for discussion later. Eventually people will realize that ratholing is a futile gesture, at least when you're running the meeting.

7. HIJACKING A MEETING

This is a more sophisticated variation of ratholing. In this case, the goal is to actively direct the meeting in a completely different direction from the one the meeting leader intends.

Here's how it works. Suppose a coworker you've invited to your meeting wants to work an issue that's not on your agenda, or that is even contrary to that agenda. The coworker decides to *hijack your meeting* for his own ends.

In preparation, the coworker suggests a list of other people who should be invited to your meeting. Before the meeting, the coworker meets privately with as many of those people as possible, obtaining their support for the coworker's agenda.

When the meeting takes place, the coworker volunteers to take minutes. The coworker's allies change the direction of the meeting to work the coworker's issues rather than yours. Then after the meeting, the coworker sends out meeting minutes that support the coworker's agenda.

There are two ways to prevent your meeting from being hijacked. First, have a clear agenda and distribute it well before the meeting. Second, either take your own minutes for your own meetings or delegate this task to somebody you trust. Then distribute your minutes immediately after the meeting, thereby preempting the would-be hijacker's minutes.

8. STEALING CREDIT

There's an old saying that goes something like this: "The king of hell is easy to avoid; it's the little demons that get you." That's certainly the case with stealing credit. The big abuses—such as somebody's sticking his or her name on something you wrote—are obvious.

It's the more subtle forms of credit-stealing that are harder to prevent. I've met people who have built *entire careers* out of worming themselves into projects that are almost complete and then hogging the limelight.

Your best defense against credit-stealing is to write and distribute ongoing progress reports whenever there's even a *possibility* that somebody might try to steal credit for your work.

That way, if there's ever controversy over who's contributed or who's responsible for the success of your project, you can simply point to your reports. The reports prevent the situation from descending into a "he said/she said" discussion.

Beyond that, you've got to be willing to publicly embarrass the person who's trying to claim credit. (Unless it's your boss, in which case you're better off keeping mum and letting your reports speak for themselves.)

For example, if you're in a meeting and somebody talks about the success of your project while implying that he or she is responsible, you *must* very quickly point out (even if you have to interrupt to do so) that the presenter wasn't really involved.

You don't have to be rude, but you do have to be straightforward. Say something like, "I just wanted to thank Steve for providing a status report on project X, but somehow the fact that it's my project got dropped from his slides."

After you've done something like this two or three times, nobody will dare attempt to steal credit from you again. The other side of this, of course, is that if you let it slide even once, the credit-stealer will know you're a pushover and steal again.

9. THROWING BANANA PEELS

This one is truly insidious. If a coworker or employee is secretly hoping you'll fail, he or she will sometimes stockpile facts or rumors that will throw you off your game at a crucial moment.

For example, right before you're about to make an important presentation to senior management, your (secretly evil) employee might tell you, "There's a rumor going around that you're addicted to painkillers. Now go in there and knock 'em dead!"

As you can well imagine, such news is so distracting that you'll find it difficult to focus and probably end up making a fool of yourself. Which is, of course, exactly what your employee wanted.

The only reason this trick is so effective is that the banana peel is being thrown by somebody you (wrongly) believe has your best interests at heart. If this kind of "news" came from an obvious enemy, you'd probably just shrug it off.

Thwarting this trick, therefore, involves identifying enemies who disguise themselves as friends. (These are the "frenemies" I identified in "Secret 11. The Ten Types of Annoying Coworker.")

With every work relationship, ask yourself, "Does this person stand to gain or lose by my success?"

Consider the question both from a business perspective (e.g., "Are we both in competition for the same promotion?") and a psychological perspective (e.g., "Does this person—or would this person—resent my success?"). For example, a coworker who expresses schadenfreude (delight in the misfortunes of others) when successful people are struck by disaster will probably be secretly delighted if you fall flat on your face.

Timing is also important. Unless there's some reason you needed to know that particular bit of information at that particular moment, assume that the true purpose of the revelation was to trip you up. A true friend would have remained mum.

SHORTCUT

DIRTY POLITICS

- ■ *DEVELOPMENT OPPORTUNITIES*: Avoid them because you're about to be used.

- ■ *ROCK FETCHES*: Your boss is avoiding a decision so force the issue.

- ■ *SACRIFICIAL LAMBS*: You're being set up so give credit where due.

- ■ *CARD-FORCING*: Two of three choices are bogus so demand new ones.

- ■ *HIDING SKELETONS*: Check the next-to-last page; don't accept gibberish.

- ■ *RATHOLING A MEETING*: Beware of subjects that distract from your agenda.

- ■ *HIJACKING A MEETING*: Don't let others "stuff" your meeting with their allies.

- ■ *STEALING CREDIT*: Document progress and publicly confront credit leeches.

- ■ *THROWING BANANA PEELS*: Ignore people or comments that throw you offtrack.

44

How to Cope with Management Fads

In some companies it's like clockwork. Every couple of years or so, somebody in the executive suite decides that what's needed to make the organization *really* productive is a new approach to managing people.

Despite what you might think, management fads aren't fads because they're something new. Quite the contrary, what makes them fads is that companies glom on to them...one after the other after the other.

Here are nine common management fads with tips to ensure you can still build your career, even while your company pursues faux panaceas.

1. SIX SIGMA

I won't go into what the six sigmas stand for, because you can look that up on the Web. Suffice it to say that the idea is to improve the quality of your processes by identifying and removing the causes of defects and errors.

In theory that's not a bad idea, but in practice Six Sigma is like a cartoon cult. It involves awarding people differently colored belts (as in a karate class) based on their expertise in the Six Sigma methodology. The result is a hierarchy of "belted" experts who run around the company pretending that they know how to do other people's work better than the people who actually do it. Endless meetings ensue, with little or no effect.

What to do? Well, if your company implements Six Sigma, expect everything to take 10 to 20 percent longer than it otherwise would because of buttinsky "experts" clogging up the way the organization runs.

This productivity tax will continue for about two years, after which everybody will gradually awaken, as if from a bad dream, put away their funny little belts, and pretend that Six Sigma never happened. So your best bet is simply to wait it out.

2. REENGINEERING

Reengineering is one of half a dozen euphemisms that executives use when they're planning to fire a bunch of people. (Some others are *downsizing, rightsizing, creative destruction, rationalizing,* and *ventilating.*)

Executives use these euphemisms because the fancy terminology makes them sound as if they're doing something impressive rather than merely laying people off, an action that is always the result of one of two things (or both):

1. *Bad planning.* The executives expanded the company too quickly, didn't understand where the market was headed, were unable to adopt required changes to the business model, and something of the sort.

2. *Predatory compensation.* Executives looking to increase the value of their stock options often fire large numbers of people because the short-term boost to profitability makes the stock price temporarily rise.

The challenge with reengineering is spotting it before it actually happens. In my experience, there are three e-mails that *always* signal that a layoff is imminent. The exact wording will vary, but they read like this:

Subject: Office Supplies
To all employees:
It has come to our attention that as a company we can all be more responsible in our use of various office supplies. For example, we purchase over 1 million paper clips every year, all of which can and should be reused.

Subject: Air Travel
To all employees:
Effective immediately, use of the corporate jet will be limited to members of the executive leadership team. Furthermore, all frequent-flier miles earned by employees will be pooled and used strictly for business travel.

Subject: Payroll Checks
To all employees:
There will be a delay in the processing of this week's payroll checks due to an unforeseen computer problem. The technical staff is working on the issue and we expect a resolution shortly.

If any of these e-mails arrives in your inbox, a "reengineering" is not far behind. If you get the third e-mail, the "reengineering" is next week.

If your company is going through, or about to go through, a round of layoffs, it's time to find another job, regardless of how well you're positioned to survive. Layoffs almost never work and almost always signal that a company is in a downward spiral. (See "Secret 39. What to Do if There's a Layoff.")

3. MATRIX MANAGEMENT

The idea here is that people with similar skills should be "pooled" for work assignments. For example, suppose you've got a group of engineers. Rather than simply have them report to a director of engineering, you also have them report to the director of marketing and a chief technology officer.

The result is predictable: an endless, debilitating turf war, where each manager fights to be considered the "real" manager by finding extra hoops to be jumped through and extra rocks to be fetched.

Productivity grinds to an immediate halt. For example, I was once employed by a firm that had a matrix management structure. As a result, people were expected to spend three hours a week in three different staff meetings, which meant wasting nine hours of every workweek.

There are other disadvantages as well. Because this system creates more managers, the organization quickly becomes top-heavy. Management becomes completely consumed by arguments over who will do what and when.

If you're determined to remain with the organization while this stupidity plays itself out, plan on spending a lot of time answering e-mails and texts while attending mind-bendingly boring meetings.

But don't despair! The concept of matrix management is inherently unstable. It only lasts until one manager wins the turf war, after which the scheme collapses, usually within six months or so. Once again, you'll need to wait it out.

4. MANAGEMENT BY CONSENSUS

Consensus management is usually seen as an alternative to the top-down decision-making common inside hierarchical organizations. In theory, important decisions are to be made with the agreement of everybody in the group.

Since everybody has a say in the decision, anybody can effectively veto any decision. As a result the only decisions that get made are those that are innocuous and support the status quo. Difficult decisions—ones that might ruffle feathers—tend to get shunted aside.

Consensus management is also subject to what's called the *Abilene paradox*: a group will unanimously agree upon a course of action that, individually, nobody wants, simply because no one is willing to go against the perceived will of the group.

The good thing about management by consensus is that it's easy to manipulate the consensus to be whatever you want. You do this by volunteering to keep minutes of all the meetings in which consensus is to be reached.

That way, when you write up the minutes for distribution, you can characterize the discussion so the consensus was that a certain decision was reached rather than just that a discussion took place. You'll thereby be providing a valuable service to the entire team.

5. CORE COMPETENCY

It sounds like good advice: focus on the single thing that your firm does better than anyone else. You will thus make your strategy difficult for competitors to imitate and keep your organization from wasting time doing things it's lousy at.

Unfortunately, organizations, just like the people inside them, tend to be as self-aware as a turnip. As a result they seldom know what they're really good at, and often believe they're wonderful in areas where they're startlingly mediocre.

More important, this management fad keeps a company locked into doing what it was successful at in the past, thereby making it less able to adapt to changing circumstances.

If the core competency fad takes hold, your only refuge is to get involved in the committee that determines the core competency. As the committee mulls the issue over, gradually migrate your allegiance (and job) to whatever part of the company looks to be winning.

6. MANAGEMENT BY OBJECTIVES

With management by objectives (aka MBO) you define objectives within an organization so that management and employees agree to them. Then you compare the employees' actual performance with the agreed-upon objectives.

On the surface there's nothing wrong with this idea. However, it becomes a fad when people turn what should be a fairly simple exercise into a paperwork nightmare. In this case the process of planning and evaluating work takes more effort than the work itself.

What's worse, explicitly laying out objectives—and basing compensation on them—makes it difficult for organizations and individuals to change gears when something unexpected happens.

The best way to deal with MBO is to use the process to negotiate the terms under which you'll get a raise or a promotion. I discuss this in "Secret 4. How to Use Your Performance Review" and "Secret 5. How to Ask for a Raise."

7. BEST PRACTICES

Since the days of Tom Peters's *In Search of Excellence*, management pundits have insisted it's possible to become successful by imitating the strategies and tactics of existing firms that are already successful.

There's only one problem: it doesn't often work. The most successful companies—Apple, Coke, IBM, P&G, etc.—tend to be one of a kind. The strategies that work (or worked) for them aren't likely to work in a different industry or for a smaller firm.

What's worse, the "successful" firms featured in "best practices" books are often past their prime anyway. *In Search of Excellence* is a case in point. Most of the companies featured in the book soon experienced horrible problems, and several went bankrupt.

Fortunately, management fads based on "best practices" always peter out when companies actually try to implement those practices. Your best approach is to slather on the lip service and proceed with business as usual.

8. STACK RANKING

This fad is truly evil. In order to improve performance every year, management awards major promotions, raises, and perks to the top 20 percent of employees, offers continuing employment to the next 70 percent, and fires the bottom 10 percent.

In theory stack ranking is supposed to create and reinforce a meritocracy. In practice it forces managers and employees to spend an enormous amount of time and effort fighting political battles.

In stack ranking organizations, managers become successful by advocating for their employees' rankings rather than by developing their potential. Employees thrive by looking good (and making others look bad) rather than by actually getting work done.

If you work for a firm that's using stack ranking, your best strategy is get assigned to a group where you'll be the star, so you'll rank at the top and thus get the rewards. Then make certain your boss knows how much better you are than everyone else.

Similarly, avoid getting assigned to a team full of talented people, because then it's more likely that somebody else will get ranked higher than you.

Long term, you probably want to get out of any company that

practices stack ranking. Companies that adopt it tend to either stall and become less innovative (Microsoft and Motorola come to mind) or turn into snake pits that tolerate all sorts of unethical behavior (such as Enron).

9. RESTRUCTURING

Restructuring, sometimes known as *reorganizing*, is the management fad that never goes out of style. Restructuring consists of the shuffling of responsibilities from one executive to another, usually accompanied by the renaming of various groups or divisions.

Executives love restructuring because it creates the illusion of bold strategic change without their actually having to change something. Many large companies restructure every year or so and they never explain why the last restructuring didn't work.

This is not to say that companies never need to restructure. Indeed, as a company grows or changes direction, it's sometimes necessary to change things up. Much of the time, though, restructuring just provides the illusion of change rather than actual change.

In most cases, restructuring is simply a manifestation of turf wars among the managers, accompanied by juicy political infighting of the "who's in and who's out" variety. The resulting turmoil makes everything grind to a halt while everyone tries to figure out what's going on, to whom they'll be reporting, and what that person is like.

Managers newly assigned after a restructuring can cause real headaches. They often feel they must assert their new authority over their new group by making some bold decisions. However, since the newbie doesn't yet understand the entire situation, these decisions are almost always bad.

When you experience a restructuring, your best bet is to ignore the political imbroglio and instead hunker down and do your job really well. Ideally, you want to be able to announce the achievement of a significant goal immediately after the new manager comes on board.

MANAGEMENT FADS

- *SIX SIGMA* creates busybodies; ignore them until they go away.

- *REENGINEERING* means layoffs; activate your escape plan.

- *MATRIX MANAGEMENT* is endless turf warfare; wait it out.

- *MANAGEMENT BY CONSENSUS* means you need to manage the "consensus."

- *CORE COMPETENCY* means one group gets favored; get yourself assigned to it.

- *MANAGEMENT BY OBJECTIVES* is paperwork; use it to document your achievements.

- *BEST PRACTICES* is imitating old strategies; praise the strategy, then ignore it.

- *STACK RANKING* creates cutthroat politics; either leave or learn to cut throats.

- *RESTRUCTURING* means a new manager; impress him by achieving a goal.

SECRET 45

How to Spot a Workplace Lie

There are two reasons it's important to identify lies. First, you naturally want to make your decisions based on reality rather than falsehood, and lies make it more difficult to make good decisions. Second, identifying lies helps you to assess the character of the people with whom you work. When you see a pattern of underhandedness, you know ahead of time that you'll be lied to and can adapt your plans accordingly.

With that in mind, there are four primary ways that people lie in the workplace:

- *Bald-faced lies.* The liar knows A to be true, but instead claims that B is true. This is the classic lie; the rest are more subtle.
- *Half-truths.* The liar technically tells the truth, but only those parts of it that will mislead the other person.
- *Indirect lies.* The liar technically tells the truth by attributing the lie to some other person or organization.
- *Bogus statistics.* The liar encapsulates a numerical truth in a way that it will probably be misconstrued. (I discuss this in "Secret 46. How to Identify a Bogus Statistic.")

1. HOW TO SPOT A BALD-FACED LIE.

Bald-faced lies come in two varieties: verbal and written.

Verbal bald-faced lies are more common than written ones because written ones leave an "audit trail" proving that the liar has lied. If a lie remains verbal, it can always be explained away as a "misunderstanding" or as part of a "he said/she said" conflict.

There are eight signs that suggest a person is telling a bald-faced lie:

1. The speaker fidgets or shows other signs of anxiety.
2. The speaker won't meet your eye.
3. The speaker overcompensates by staring into your eyes.
4. The speaker's story sounds overly rehearsed.
5. The speaker changes the story over time.
6. The speaker insists that he or she is telling the truth.
7. The speaker has an excellent reason to lie.
8. The speaker has told lies in the past.

When the bald-faced lie is written, rather than spoken, only signs 5 through 8 apply. In both cases the rule of thumb is: *trust your gut.* If it feels as if you're hearing a lie, you probably are.

2. HOW TO SPOT A HALF-TRUTH.

People tell half-truths because they want all the benefits of telling a lie (i.e., mislead you to their advantage) without the risk of being caught out or suffering the burden of being forced to think of themselves as liars.

For example, suppose your boss knows for certain that you'll soon be laid off, but needs you to finish up your current project. If you ask, "Is my job secure?" your boss can tell the truth ("No") or a bald-faced lie ("Yes").

For your boss, though, there's a downside to both approaches. On the one hand, the truth might cause you to leave the company before your current project is complete. On the other hand, telling the bald-faced lie forces the boss to self-identify as a liar.

Because of this, the boss is more likely to tell a truth that's misleading, such as "Rest assured, your contribution is appreciated." Hearing this half-truth, you might conclude (wrongly) that your job is secure.

The trick to spotting a half-truth is to corner the possible liar and ask questions so it's more difficult for the other person to maintain the half-truth in the no-man's-land between honesty and dishonesty.

Building on the example above, suppose Fred knows that Jill is going to be laid off, but still wants her to plug away at a major project. Here's how the conversation starts:

- *Jill*: Is my job secure?
- *Fred*: Rest assured, your contribution is appreciated.

If Jill accepts this answer, she'll assume that she isn't going to be laid off. Instead, she should ask the question again, but leaving Fred less wiggle room.

- *Jill*: That's great. Am I going to be laid off?

At this point Fred must either tell the truth ("Yes") or a bald-faced lie ("I don't know"). If it's a bald-faced lie, it's likely that Fred's body language will change enough to warn Jill that she's being lied to.

Of course, Fred could simply tell another half-truth:

- *Fred*: The final decisions haven't been made.

However, by making another ambiguous statement, Fred has provided Jill with a touchstone. Rule of thumb: two ambiguous responses in a row means that the other person is lying. (In other words, two half-truths equal one full lie.)

When employees tell half-truths to their bosses, it's usually an attempt to hedge. The employee gives an answer that sounds affirmative, but has one or more caveats hidden inside it. For example:

- *Jill (boss)*: Are you going to complete this project on time?
- *Jim (engineer)*: Yes, the technicians will finish the testing on Monday.

But just a moment! How can Jim possibly know if his project will finish on time when he doesn't yet know the test results? Therefore, Jim's yes is a half-truth that should signal Jill to press the point further.

- *Jill*: What if the tests are negative?

Identifying people who tell half-truths allows you to assess whether they can be trusted and whether you can believe their promises and commitments, which allows you to make better decisions.

3. HOW TO SPOT AN INDIRECT LIE.

An indirect lie happens when somebody passes along information that he or she knows is untrue, by claiming he heard that piece of information from somebody else.

For example, Fred knows a layoff is imminent, but when asked about it says, "Jerry doesn't think so." Fred may technically be telling the truth (because Jerry is misinformed), but the statement is intended to mislead.

Here's another example. You can turn almost any false statement into something that's technically true by preceding it with the phrase "It's rumored that…" Such statements are always "true" because the statement *starts the rumor.*

To spot an indirect lie, poke at the source that the possible liar is citing. If you find it wanting, ask the question again more directly. For example:

- *Jill*: Is a layoff coming?
- *Fred*: Jerry doesn't think so.
- *Jill*: And is Jerry in a position to know for certain?
- *Fred*: Uh...maybe...
- *Jill*: To the best of your knowledge, is a layoff coming?

Once again you've maneuvered Fred into a position in which he must tell either the truth or a bald-faced lie.

SHORTCUT

WORKPLACE LIES

- **LIARS** reveal themselves by their body language.
- **LIARS** are often overly insistent that they're telling the truth.
- **HALF-TRUTHS** are technically true but intended to mislead.
- **FLUSH** out half-truths by pressing for specifics.
- **INDIRECT** lies attribute the lie to somebody not present.
- **FLUSH** out indirect lies by questioning the source.

How to Identify a Bogus Statistic

Mark Twain wrote, "There are three kinds of lies: lies, damned lies, and statistics." Since statistics are traded around the workplace with gusto, it's in your interest to be able to identify the ones that misrepresent the truth. To do this, ask these five questions:

1. IS THE DATA SOURCE OBJECTIVE?

Statistics are only as valid as the data that lies behind them. As a general rule, if the person or organization that gathers the data will receive some kind of financial benefit if the data is skewed, the data will be skewed.

For example, if a corporation responsible for a large amount of pollution funds a study "proving" that the pollution is harmless, the data in that study is almost guaranteed to be skewed, because otherwise the polluter would be forced to spend money to clean it up.

2. IS THE SAMPLING RANDOM?

Companies frequently run Web polls in which people accessing the website decide whether they want to participate in the survey.

However, any statistics based on these "self-selected" polls are automatically bogus.

For example, if I stick on a website a question like, "How well are we doing on customer service?" only people who have had very good or very bad customer service experiences will bother to answer. You'll have no idea what the typical customer thinks.

3. DOES IT MISUSE THE CONCEPT OF AN AVERAGE?

Many bogus statistics use averages in a way that's clearly intended to mislead. For example, in a room with one billionaire and 999 people who are penniless, the average wealth per person is a million dollars. While true, the statistic is misleading.

Rather than averages, valid statistics tend to use the concept of a *median*, which is the middle value when all values are arranged in order. In the example above, the median wealth per person is zero dollars, regardless of the presence of the billionaire.

4. DOES IT ASSUME CAUSALITY?

Even if two sets of data seem to be in lockstep, you have no idea whether that is meaningful until you know for certain that one thing caused the other. Correlation is not causation.

For example, if your sales revenue spikes upward after your salespeople attend a sales training class, the increased revenue *may* be the result of sales training or *may* be the result of something unrelated, like an improvement in economic conditions.

5. IS THE GRAPHIC REASONABLE?

Graphical presentations of data (whether bogus or real) can also mislead. For example, by tweaking the scale of a graph, you can make a small difference look like a big difference (or vice versa):

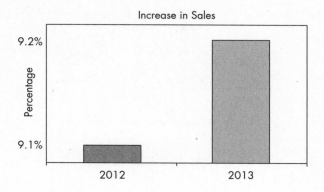

The graphic gives the impression that there's been a huge increase in sales, when in fact, sales increased only by a measly .1 percent. Rule of thumb: the fancier the graphs, the more likely it is that the presentation is purposefully misleading.

Another way to distort graphics is to present insignificant amounts in a way that makes them seem significant. For example, if you ask nine customers a question and eight of them answer yes, you create a graphic like this:

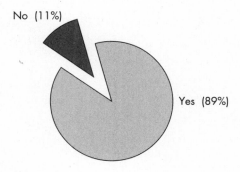

However, if you've got thousands of customers, it's impossible that those nine are representative of your entire customer base. You end up with a statistic that seems authoritative but is in fact entirely bogus.

BOGUS STATISTICS

■ **IF** the data source makes money on the statistic, the data is probably bogus.

■ **IF** the people surveyed volunteered to be surveyed, the statistic is meaningless.

■ **THE** concept of an average is often abused; ask, "What's the median?"

■ **WHEN** things happen in parallel they're not necessarily related.

■ **GRAPHICS** tend to make statistics appear more significant than they are.

The Eight Lies Most Bosses Tell

The boss/employee relationship has an inherent inequality of power, and since knowledge is power, most bosses will want to keep some knowledge to themselves and away from employees. Doing so often involves telling the following lies:

1. "WE CAN'T PAY YOU MORE."

The crux of this lie is located in the word *can't*. If a company has any cash flow whatsoever, the boss is making decisions about where to spend based on what the boss feels is a priority. Your salary isn't the priority, so *can't* really means *won't*.

Ideally, of course, compensation should be comparable, at least in some sense, to the amount of value each employee creates. Because that's seldom the case, bosses are often forced to lie to employees in order to keep from being pressured to pay more.

Since your compensation always reflects the minimum your boss believes you'll accept, when you hear this lie, it's a signal that you need to renegotiate the compensation agreement you have with your boss. (See "Secret 5. How to Ask for a Raise.")

2. "YOUR RAISE IS ABOVE AVERAGE."

If you're in an organization in which the compensation for everyone in the group is pulled from a set amount of money, there's a good chance that the boss is describing almost everyone's raise as "above average."

Companies that employ nonunion labor are exquisitely sensitive about anybody sharing salary information, because such sharing inevitably makes somebody feel that he or she is being slighted. Bosses therefore tell this lie because they're afraid that if you knew what your coworkers were being paid, you would quit in disgust. To discover whether the claim is actually a lie, push for further details. (See "Secret 45. How to Spot a Workplace Lie.")

3. "WE'RE ONE BIG HAPPY FAMILY."

In real life happy families don't keep secrets from one another, and tend to share everything equally. Since that isn't the case with any business, the only kind of family a business can resemble is a highly dysfunctional one.

Indeed, the most wretched places to work are those in which bosses and employees replicate the yelling, spanking, criticism, deception, and cruelty that play a huge role in the horrors of a miserable childhood.

Bosses tell this lie in the hope that you'll feel reluctant to push for a raise or promotion lest you upset "your family." Therefore, your best bet is to quietly refuse the entire premise of the lie and remember that it's not personal, it's business.

4. "THERE'S NO TRUTH TO THE LAYOFF RUMOR."

This statement means that a layoff is definitely going to happen. This lie is told because management either wants to keep the talented people from jumping ship or wants to prevent irate employees from committing acts of vandalism before they're escorted to the door.

Before you get too irritated at your boss for telling you this whopper, consider that your boss is probably fighting for his or her own career, is being asked to do top management's dirty work, and may end up being the last person to get axed.

The moment you hear your boss deny *any* rumor, you immediately know that it's true. Therefore, if you hear this one, you should immediately activate your escape plan. (See "Secret 39. What to Do If There's a Layoff.")

5. "MY HANDS ARE TIED."

Bosses feign helplessness when they want to renege on a commitment to an employee, or escape blame for a decision that's unfavorable to the employee. Example: "I tried hard to get you the raise I promised you, but since sales are down, my hands are tied."

By attributing the decision to corporate policy or salary guidelines, the boss not only escapes your ire, but can leave you feeling as if you owe the boss for at least "trying" to get you what you want.

However, there are always exceptions to policies and guidelines, but they require effort on the part of your boss to make them happen. Therefore, rather than giving up when you hear this lie, push harder for what you want.

6. "YOU'LL BE WORKING FORTY HOURS A WEEK."

If your boss thinks of your work in terms of the hours you expend on the job, and you are *not* paid by the hour (that is, you're salaried), your boss will constantly pressure you to work more than forty hours a week.

This is simple economics. The only reason any company turns an hourly job into a salaried position is that it's then possible to extract more time from each worker than the company is paying for.

Whenever you hear this lie, assume that you'll be pressured to work unpaid overtime. Not to worry, though. If you treat this demand as unreasonable (see "Secret 6. How to Handle Unreasonable Requests"), you can get out of working unpaid overtime. Then, if you manage your time correctly, you'll get more done than the people who are coerced into working ridiculously long hours. (See "Secret 23. How to Have Enough Time.")

7. "YOUR RESPONSE WILL BE CONFIDENTIAL."

This lie is generally told when employees are asked to participate in a survey that solicits criticism of the company or its management. The hope is that employees will truthfully communicate their negative opinions and views.

The moment you sign an employee contract, however, you waive your right to privacy. So if you're asked for a confidential opinion, your best bet is to "praise with faint damnation," even if you're being surveyed by a supposedly "independent" source.

For example, if you're asked "confidentially" if your boss is doing a good job, don't say something like, "He's in over his head." Such honesty will come back and bite you, so say something innocuous like, "My boss works too hard."

8. "YOUR PARTICIPATION IS VOLUNTARY."

This lie always means its opposite. For example, attendance at a "brown-bag lunch" where top management will be giving a presentation is voluntary only if you plan to voluntarily get fired.

Similarly, you're putting your job at great risk if you don't "voluntarily" contribute to the annual charity drive. As the great historian Edward Gibbon put it: "The invitations of a master are scarcely to be distinguished from commands."

In the corporate world, *voluntary* is code for *mandatory*. Whenever you're told that something is voluntary, always be the first person to sign up and the last person to complain about it.

COMMON BOSS LIES

- *"WE CAN'T PAY YOU MORE."* Truth: your salary isn't a priority.

- *"YOUR RAISE IS ABOVE AVERAGE."* Truth: you probably got stiffed.

- *"WE'RE ONE BIG HAPPY FAMILY."* Truth: this place is totally dysfunctional.

- *"THERE'S NO TRUTH TO THE LAYOFF RUMOR."* Truth: a layoff is **imminent**.

- *"MY HANDS ARE TIED."* Truth: I'm unwilling to fight for what you want.

- *"YOU'LL BE WORKING FORTY HOURS A WEEK."* Truth: you will have no personal life.

- *"YOUR RESPONSE WILL BE CONFIDENTIAL."* Truth: it will be used against you.

- *"YOUR PARTICIPATION IS VOLUNTARY."* Truth: your participation is mandatory.

48

The Seven Times It's OK to Lie to the Boss

At first glance this chapter might seem to run contrary to the overall theme of this book, because lies increase rather than decrease the amount of bullsh*t in the workplace.

However, there is a social contract between human beings: don't lie to me and I won't lie to you. In business that contract is often seen as working only one way: a boss can lie but an employee cannot. And that's the real bullsh*t.

When bosses tell self-serving lies about salaries, raises, layoffs, work hours, etc., they set themselves beyond the limits of ethical human behavior. That being the case, they no longer have any right to ask for total honesty from the people they employ.

Of course, you may always *choose* to tell the truth, but in the circumstances below... lying may be the better part of candor.

1. WHEN LYING IS PART OF YOUR JOB.

Some jobs, by definition, involve fooling the public with half-truths. If that's the case with your job, you'd best be consistent in private. Trust me, if your boss hired you to lie, the last thing he or she wants is to be told the truth.

For example, suppose you're responsible for public relations at an oil company. Admitting to your boss that you know you're spouting nonsense about global warming makes you look like a hypocrite. If you must lie as part of your job, it's also your job to lie consistently.

2. WHEN YOU'RE PROTECTING COWORKERS.

If you have personal dirt on your coworkers, you owe it to them to keep it to yourself, even if the boss asks. For example, if you're aware that Joe called in sick because he was drinking whiskey until 3 a.m. the night before, your best response is "I have no idea why he's not here."

The same thing goes for various screwups that are outside your realm of responsibility. Even if you know who's to blame, it's not your job to be the office tattletale. The number one rule of business is to mind your own.

3. WHEN YOU'RE ACTIVELY JOB HUNTING.

If it gets out that you're looking, you might be penalized with either a loss of status or a loss of power. You might even get fired before you find the job you want.

You have a right to look for another job without suffering unpleasant consequences, so feel free to tell any lies you must to keep your job search secret. Trust me, if your boss were looking for another job, he or she would do the same.

4. WHEN YOUR BOSS TELLS A LAME JOKE.

Being a boss means that underlings must laugh at your jokes, even when they're awful. If you're the underling, despite your having heard that joke for the tenth time, and its not having been funny the first, you must emit an appreciative chuckle.

Yeah, it's a bit degrading, but think of it this way: at least your boss is trying to be entertaining. It's probably a good idea to encourage any attempt on the part of a boss to lighten things up a little. So laugh; it's not going to break your face.

5. WHEN YOUR BOSS SHOOTS MESSENGERS.

When bosses punish people for telling uncomfortable truths, they're communicating that they do not want to be told such truths. For example, a CEO who berates a sales manager for providing a realistic sales forecast is asking to be told a lie ("Sales will be *up!*").

The only time you should communicate hard truths to this type of boss is *after* you've accepted a job somewhere else. Indeed, if your boss is shooting messengers, your number one job should be finding another boss.

6. WHEN YOUR BOSS NEEDS PLAUSIBLE DENIABILITY.

You're not helping your boss when you communicate a truth that puts him or her into such a position that he or she must lie in order to keep from being fired, or to prevent your team's budget from being cut.

Here's the magic question: "Do you *really* want to know the truth?" If your boss says something like, "No, not really," you're being asked to keep your mouth shut. As long as doing so isn't actually unethical, you should definitely comply.

7. WHEN IT'S NONE OF THE BOSS'S DAMN BUSINESS.

If your boss decides to quiz you on your religion, your politics, your personal life, your sexual orientation, your eating habits, what you smoke, or anything else that doesn't directly affect your work performance, you have no obligation to answer the question.

In situations such as this you can't politely decline to answer, because your refusal to answer is itself an answer. Instead you should feel free to tell the boss whatever you think he or she would like to hear.

In most areas of the world, corporations are allowed to monitor everything you do. They can even demand blood tests, which means they can "own" a part of your physical body. So cling like crazy to your last remaining shreds of privacy...even if it means fibbing.

SHORTCUT

YOU CAN LIE TO YOUR BOSS WHEN . . .

- ...your job entails lying to the public.
- ...the boss wants you to rat out your coworkers.
- ...you're actively looking for another job.
- ...the boss cracks a bad joke (laugh anyway).
- ...the boss punishes people who tell the truth.
- ...the boss really, really needs you to keep the truth private.
- ...the boss pries into your private life.

How to Safely Be a Whistle-Blower

Finally, here's a situation that I hope you are never forced to deal with: what to do if you discover that your company has done something unethical or illegal. In this case, you have four choices:

1. *Shrug and forget about it.* As long as you're not going to be arrested yourself, why should you care?

2. *Quit and forget about it.* Get out so your career isn't damaged. Afterward, why should you care?

3. *Become a public whistle-blower.* You expose the malfeasance, lose your job, and in all probability destroy your career.

4. *Become a private whistle-blower.* You expose the malfeasance while leaving yourself out of the picture, without damage to your career.

This chapter will focus on the fourth alternative, hence the word *safely* in the title.

1. ASK, "WILL IT REALLY MAKE A DIFFERENCE?"

Publicly held corporations are natural sociopaths. They are legally bound to their stockholders to make the most profit possible, even if doing so involves robbery, slavery, environmental destruction, and the death of innocents, including children.

There are only two ways to restrain corporations from sociopathic behavior. The first is to pass laws and enact government regulation that increases the cost of these behaviors so they become less profitable. The second is to publicize these behaviors in such a way that customers, investors, and employees avoid the corporation, simply to escape the taint.

Unfortunately, many governments are hand in glove with business interests and therefore create massive loopholes that allow corporations to avoid fines and arrests that might negatively affect profit.

Similarly, the public has become exceedingly tolerant of horrible corporate behaviors, providing it, the public, is not the direct victim and so long as it, the public, gets the benefit of lower prices.

Therefore, the first question you should ask yourself, before becoming a whistle-blower, is whether anyone really cares. If blowing the whistle isn't going to change anything, why bother?

2. CONSIDER YOUR POSITION.

Assuming you've gotten this far, the dumbest thing you can do is to bring the matter to the attention of your boss, your boss's boss, your boss's peers, or anybody else in authority at your company.

Chances are *they already know all about it*. In fact, your management is probably expending all sorts of mental and emotional energy *not* thinking about the situation that you're about to throw in their faces.

Any attempt to deal with unethical corporate behavior through official corporate channels will result in a loss of your status and very possibly the loss of your job. Even if it doesn't, you're now marked as *the* whistle-blower, even if somebody else ends up blowing the whistle.

It gets worse. Now that you've identified yourself as a trouble-maker, you'll be marked as somebody who can't be trusted. Your managers may even try to set you up to take blame if the secret gets out.

If what you want to expose is heinous enough, the sacrifice may be worth it. However, consider whether you truly want to be a martyr. If so, maybe being a whistle-blower is more about your needs than about those of whoever would be helped. Just something to think about.

3. GATHER INCRIMINATING DATA.

Let's suppose you've decided to go forward. What's needed now is data that proves the unethical behavior is actually taking place, with the knowledge of those who could have stopped it (i.e., management).

As you gather this data, your main goal is to keep your fingerprints (digital and otherwise) off everything you gather. This can be difficult because your company can probably track back to you everything that happens on your computer or your phone.

For example, if you forward an incriminating e-mail to a government agency, the e-mail contains hidden information that can tie it back to you. Same thing if you take photos on your cell phone.

And make no mistake about it, there's probably *somebody* in the government agency who will share with your management that you were the source of the incriminating data. This is not paranoia, but simply a recognition of how things work in the real world.

Therefore, the only safe way to gather incriminating information is to put it through an analog step that destroys any hidden digital identifying information. This means using only photocopies and photoprints.

4. LEAVE, THEN LEAK.

Now that you've gathered the incriminating evidence, it's time to leave before everything blows up, because if you remain, I absolutely guarantee you're the one who's going to be damaged.

Hopefully, the moment you realized you were working for ~~criminals~~ the ethically challenged, you started looking for another job in a company that doesn't share the same business model as your current employer.

Wait at least two months after you've left the company. Anonymously send copies of the material you gathered to any of the following that are relevant:

- News sources that do exposés (they do still exist).
- Government agencies with authority over the malfeasance.
- Law enforcement agencies responsible for policing these crimes.

Take the *anonymous* part of *anonymously* seriously. Mail the material from a post office far from where you currently live and/or work so the postmark doesn't suggest you might be involved. Do *not* include a way to get in contact with you.

If the reporter, government official, or law enforcer has skills at all, he or she will be able to use the material you provided to find out more. Warning: no matter how careful you've been, there's a good chance you'll be outed.

SHORTCUT

BLOWING THE WHISTLE

- **BLOW** the whistle only if it will truly make a difference.
- **IF** you complain directly to management you'll suffer.
- **SECRETLY** gather documentation of the abuse.
- **LEAVE** the company before you leak the documents.

Acknowledgments

This book exists only because of my agent Lorin Rees, who encouraged me to develop the concept, and my editor Gretchen Young; Rick Wolff, publisher of Business Plus; and assistant editor Allyson Rudolph. They helped me hone the message of this book into something more original and pertinent.

I also owe a debt of gratitude to the excellent and talented editors I've worked with at Inc.com: Nicole Carter, Rachel Elson, Nicole Richardson, and Editor in Chief Eric Schurenberg, who brought me along when he moved from CBS to Inc.com.

There are some people who deserve special recognition:

The chapter about annoying coworkers grew out of a series of blog posts that riffed on Sylvia Lafair's excellent book *Don't Bring It to Work: Breaking the Family Patterns That Limit Success*. The categories in this book are based on my own experience, but the idea of segmenting coworkers in this way comes from Sylvia.

Similarly, the chapter on dirty office politics, though based almost entirely on my own experience, is indebted to Mike Phipps and Colin Gautrey, whose book *21 Dirty Tricks at Work: How to Beat the Game of Office Politics* reminded me of all the times I fell for those tricks when I was first starting out. In addition, the chapter about lying with statistics has its roots in Darrell Huff and Irving Geis's classic *How to Lie with Statistics*.

The chapter on working a room is based on ideas about elevator pitches that Barry Rhein shared with me. My thoughts on coaching are heavily influenced by Linda Richardson. Art Mortell taught me about coping with rejection, which is wisdom that's reflected throughout this book.

The chapter on management fads owes a lot to my pal Jeff Pratt, who regularly fills me in on the management activity inside the company in which he's worked for the past quarter century (a significant achievement on his part).

As always, my copy editor Lauren Ruiz of Pure-text.net has been helpful in reading drafts and providing suggestions and corrections.

My friends Larry Jacobs, David Rotman, and Gerhard Gschwandtner have provided encouragement and inspiration throughout this process, as have my wonderful wife, Natalie, and my equally wonderful children, Alexander and Cordelia.

The following subscribers to my newsletter were kind enough to review the draft during the writing process: Katja Ahokas, Ann-Marie Antic, John Banks, Cat Barnard, Iain M. Bates, Kim Blair, Kevin Boswell, Gustavo Brum, Paul Burkhardt, Yvonne Burns, Sara Byfield, Vito Carrozoo, Bernard Chege, Leslie Clements, Larry Coppenrath, Michelle Craft, Nathan Craven, Lori Crider, Tim Cromwell, Otmara Diaz-Cooper, Troy Draper, Laura Carrington Duckett, Ahma Duranai, Stephen Eltze, Jonathan Fearon, Kirstie Fiora, Olivier Fontana, Sue Garvan, Henry Gertcher, John Giartonia, Nicole Green, Steve Hamburg, Paul Herring, Rob Hill, Peg Hosky, Mary Hume, Lori Humphrey, Kathi Hunt, Franklyn R. Jarine, Tanya Jovan, Brian Keller, Wayne Killns, Pat Kinnison, Professor Linda Maria Koldau, Kevin Land, Lorelie Lewis, Lorenzo Martelletti, Dale Martin, Ryan McCartney, Bob McIntyre, Grant McNulty, Srinath Mitragotri, James Napier, Samuel Nebel, Jim Newkirk, Eric Noack, Tom Nosal, Ivo Oltmans, Dawen Peng, Christer Pyyhtia, Stephanie Quaile, Stephen Revel, Tony Roach, Ray Roberts, Lanny Rootenberg, John Rowe, George Scherma, David Schmidt, Lauren Selikoff, Eric Shefferman, Dan Spacek, Alex Spletter, Confidence Stimpson, Andrei Stoica, Jakub Szrodt, Tim Taggart, Lauren Talbot, Adam Tillman, Paul Troisi, Lee Tucker, Susan Tyson, Lahat Tzvi, Rick Valdeserri, James Vos, Ryan Waterstradt, Troy Williams, Steve Windham, and Tad Woolley.

Finally, this book is dedicated to the millions of readers of my blog whose selection of posts to go viral helps me hone my ideas and understand what people really need to know to be successful.

—Geoffrey James

About the Author

Geoffrey James's award-winning blog has appeared on CBS Interactive and Inc.com. His writing has also appeared in *Fast Company*, *Wired*, *Men's Health*, and the *New York Times*.